EGYPT

Man perishes, his body returns to dust,
all his fellow creatures fall to earth,
but through the written word
his memory shall live on in men's tongues.

A book is worth more than a fine house,
more than a stele set in a sanctuary,
. . . the wise prophets have passed away,
and their names would have been forgotten
had not their writings preserved their memory.

(From the Chester Beatty IX Papyrus, New Kingdom)

EGYPT

Text by Cérès Wissa Wassef

Photographs by Albano Guatti
Design by Gianfranco Cavaliere

Scala Books, New York
distributed by Harper & Row, Publishers

Library of Congress
Catalog Card Number
83-060747

First published
in the U.S. and Canada 1983 by
Scala Books, New York

ISBN 0-935748-53-9

Project Director
Thekla Clark

Consultant
Nebojša Tomašević

Translation
Jacqueline Morley
*(Introduction, Pharaonic Egypt
and Christian Egypt)*
Paul Blanchard
(Islamic Egypt and Modern Egypt)

Produced by Scala

Printed in Milan, Italy by
Amilcare Pizzi Arti Grafiche, S.p.A.
for Scala Books
342 Madison Avenue
New York, N.Y. 10020

All photographs are by Albano Guatti
except: 67, 80, 85-89, 94, 99 by
Scala, Florence.

Endpapers: Detail from the
Book of the Dead. Turin,
Egyptian Museum.

Contents

MEDITERRANEAN
Gaza
Damietta
Port Said
Rosetta
ALEXANDRIA
Suez Canal
El Alamein
Ismailia
LOWER EGYPT
Heliopolis
CAIRO
Giza
Suez
Kattara Depression
WADI NATRUN
Sakkara
Memphis
SINAI PENINSULA
Lake Qarun
Dahshur
Fayyum
Siwa Oasis
Beni Suef
St Antony
St Paul
Gulf of Suez
St Catherine
Mt St Catherine
Gulf of Aqaba
Bahariya Oasis
Nile
MIDDLE EGYPT
El Minya
Beni Hassan
Tell-el-Amarna
ARABIAN DESERT
Orgada
Asyut
LIBYAN DESERT
Farafra Oasis
UPPER EGYPT
Sohag
Nile
Qena
RED SEA
Abydos
Dendera
Valley
of the Kings
Karnak
Luxor
Thebes
Dakhla Oasis
Hierakonpolis
Edfu
Kharga Oasis
Kom Ombo
Elephantine
Island
First cataract
ASWAN DAM
Aswan
Philae
Island
Lake Nasser
LOWER NUBIA
administrative
boundary
Nile
Gilf Kebir Plateau
Abu Simbel
political boundary

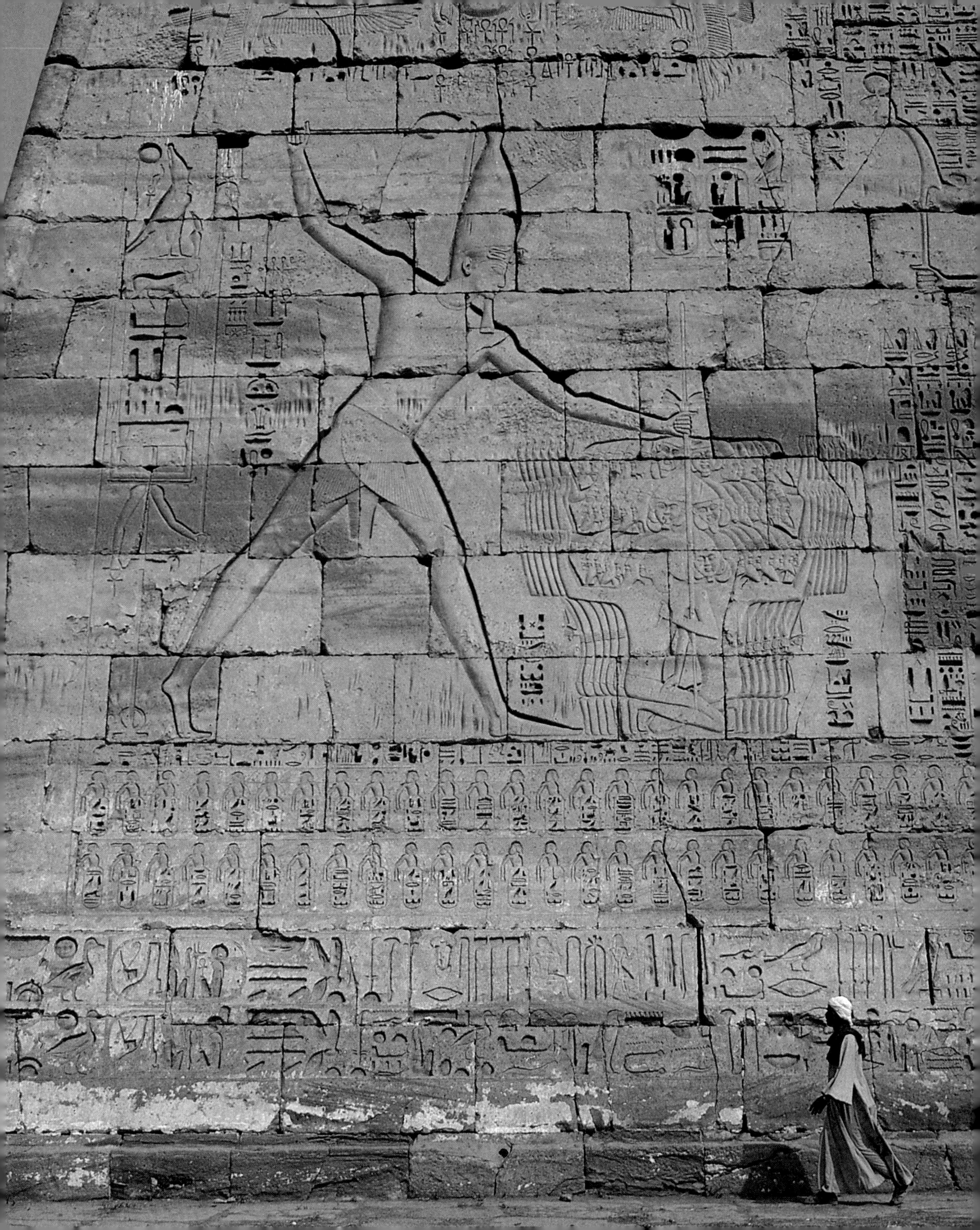

2

1. The Temple of Ramses III at Medinet Habu, on the west bank at Thebes. It is the best preserved of the New Kingdom temples.

2. The Sphinx and the Pyramids of Giza. Known in classical times as one of the seven wonders of the world, the pyramids of Cheops and Khephren are over 200 metres high.

3. View from the top of Mount Saint Catherine, in the Sinai peninsula.

4. A caravan of camels in the desert. Gustave Flaubert wrote of the camel: "that strange animal who walks as clumsily as a turkey, but sways his neck as gracefully as a swan."

5. The mosque of Ibn Tulun, built in the late ninth century, is the earliest of the great Cairo mosques.

6. Fishermen on the Nile between the old dam and the new dam at Aswan.

7. The shops in the older parts of Cairo are open onto the road and have no secrets for the passersby.

8. The minarets of the Sultan Hassan and El Rifai mosques in Cairo.

Introduction

The etymology of the name "Egypt," coming through Latin from the Greek *Aegyptos*, is obscure; it seems likely that the Greeks derived it from *Hitupah* (residence of the "Ka" of Ptah), one of the names of Memphis, then the chief port of the Nile. The Asian peoples used the name *Misr*, still used by Arab countries to denote Egypt. The ancient Egyptians called it *Kemi*, the land of black earth, bountiful provider of nourishment.

Has the prophecy of Aesculapius, Greek god of medicine, been fulfilled? "Egypt, Egypt, of your cults nothing will remain; they will become mere fables and your children will no longer believe in them. Nothing will survive but graven stones recording your greatness." Fortunately for us the Greeks themselves greatly admired Egyptian civilisation, and often acknowledged the extent of their debt to it; they assimilated much of its heritage and made good use of it.

Today, thanks to the discovery by a Frenchman, Jean-François Champollion (1790-1832), of the secret of Egyptian writing, which had been lost since the sixth century AD, we are better equipped to explore the character of ancient Egypt. We find an infinite richness and an outstanding originality, deeply infused with the comprehensive ideal of humanity which was developed by her sages.

We are able today to restore the "mother of the world," as her people call her, to the position to which her amazing contribution to our civilisation entitles her.

To what does Egypt owe the "stupendous originality" of which the experts speak? It was doubtless due to the interaction of her national temperament with the inexorable pressure of nature, whose demands determined both the economic and political structure of the country.

A unique geographical setting

Nature has given Egypt an exceptional geography. The country forms an almost perfect square (1024 km from north to south, 1240 km from east to west, about one million square km) in the north-east corner of the African continent, presenting two paradoxical characteristics. At one and the same time it is a huge oasis closed upon itself, and also a passage-way linking several continents. Egypt is the creation of the Nile; through many ages the river has patiently carved a way through the desert, to deposit its layers of silt in the dry gulf created by the shrinking of the Mediterranean, which at one time extended beyond the present site of Cairo. Its strange valley, 1000 km long but rarely more than 30 km wide, unrolls like a papyrus. It extends into a huge delta, 250 km across at it widest point, with vast lagoons persisting in the north – the lakes Mareotis, Burlus, Edku and Menzala. In its entirety the valley makes up only 4% of the country's total area (the equivalent in size of Belgium). On both sides it is surrounded by vast tracts of desert: to the east the Arabian desert, dry mountainous and inhospitable, peopled by nomadic tribes, to the west a string of fertile oases that lie on the line of a former river. Linked to the valley on its western flank by a natural arm of the Nile is a huge basin that forms the province of Fayyum, the orchard of Egypt. Such is the land which the ancient Egyptians called "the Black and the Red."

Egypt's exceptional configuration, which protected her from outside influences, very strongly contributed to a state of splendid isolation. For nearly three thousand years this isolation encouraged the development of a civilisation of astounding originality and coherence.

Egypt, situated at the crossing of so many routes, linking the Mediterranean with the Sahara, black Africa and the Near East, could not avoid becoming the object of greed and conquest. Twice occupied by the Persians – in the sixth and the fourth centuries BC – and conquered in 332 BC by Alexander the Great, she became a province of the Roman, Byzantine, Arab and Ottoman Empires; not for two thousand years was she to regain her political autonomy.

A gift of the Nile

Another geographical constraint is Egypt's dependence on the Nile. Rising at the equator from vast inland seas, this unique river collects the waters of the Sudanese grasslands and the torrents of Abyssinia; it then crosses the steppes of Nubia and enters a desert region where rapids interrupt its slow waters, cutting islands and islets in the rock. Next come six waterfalls, of which the last, at Aswan, marks the entry into Egypt. The ancient Egyptians were well aware that their country was the gift of this "primordial and tutelary force"; they knew also that its beneficent waters had to be governed. From prehistoric times they had addressed themselves to the task, levelling the ground to gain new land, cutting drainage and irrigation channels and altering their disposition as necessity dictated. To insure that the whole land obtained equal benefit it was divided into "irrigation basins" surrounded by dykes; when the flood came gaps were made in the dykes and later filled again. After about twenty days, when the waters had subsided, tilling and sowing could begin.

From Neolithic times to the end of the eighteenth century the valley had been irrigated by this method. Its circulatory system of canals, carrying life-blood throughout the land, enabled Egypt to develop a system which provided both for day to day needs and for a planned agricultural economy. The year had three seasons of equal length: the flood, the seedtime and the harvest. The floodtime was a period of inactivity: the villages, standing out as islands above the flooded countryside, could communicate only by boat, and time was passed in fishing and handicrafts. Subsequent seasons were intensely active. If the flood was too low the country was threatened by famine; if it was too high it exacted the organised labour of many thousands of workers. Hence the need for co-ordinated measurements of the river's strength and regular dispersal of its waters.

Centralisation and bureaucracy

To meet these needs a centralised and well organised state was essential. This was supplied by an administrative hierarchy which controlled every person's actions and regulated the entire economy. Its origins go back to the Old Kingdom (2778-2263 BC). Pharaoh, son and heir of the gods, himself a god, enjoyed limitless power. This power he delegated to the head of all administration – the vizier, to whom on his investiture he made this injunction: "Look well to the office of vizier . . . Keep watch over all that must be done, for it is through this office that the life of the whole land is maintained." This was, indeed, an onerous task – to direct the flow and use of water, to keep the land register and tax records, to surpervise the harvest and fill the granaries, to administer justice and maintain the prisons, to regulate the life of the court, to run the temple estates, to attend to the building of monuments and of ships, to look after the army and maintain the frontiers, to organise trading and diplomatic links with foreign powers . . . All specialists agree that it was due to this system of organisation that Egypt achieved such prosperity and was able to develop a civilisation so intellectually and technically advanced.

"Bureaucracy and pharaonic grandeur," wrote the Egyptologist Jean Yoyotte, "are one and the same."

But there is another side to the coin. After the colonial acquisitions of the New Kingdom (1580-1083 BC) the administration grew in size and complexity. Its legacy of bureaucratic obfuscation is still with us today and seriously impedes the progress of the country.

The inventors of writing

The oldest written characters which have come down to us are more than 5,000 years old. Egypt created writing independently but almost simultaneously with Mesopotamia. She did this at one stroke, without abortive experiment, and it is in this that the "miracle of Egypt" consists. Champollion describes hieroglyphics (the Greek word for "sacred images") as "a complex system, a writing at once figurative, symbolic and phonetic, in the same text, in the same phrase, almost in the same word." The hieroglyphic system reflects the two most important characteristics of ancient Egyptian civilisation: a yearning for immortality and a faith in the magical property of the written word. The essential function of the signs cut in stone was to ensure immortality for the things represented; the writing of a name or a list of provisions needed in the after-life sufficed to give them perpetual life. This power could be for good or ill, which explains why certain signs were deliberately mutilated by the scribes to rob them of the power to harm the deceased. Apart from their magical properties the signs were conceived as images to delight the eye; their ordering made a true work of art.

From the time of the Old Kingdom the stone-cut characters, used to immortalise the gods and the dead, were supplemented by a simplified cursive script, derived from hieroglyphics but dealing with the living. This *hieratic* script ("sacred writings" in Greek), was used in matters of religion, in administration and the law, in teaching and in literature. Towards the seventh century BC this gave way to a more developed cursive: the *demotic* script (in Greek, "people's writing") which was used by lawyers and officials. Finally a fourth script was evolved: the *Coptic* derived from popular dialects of ancient Egyptian, written in Greek characters. Seven demotic characters were added to the twenty-five letters of the Greek alphabet to represent sounds not occurring in that language. This simplified script was written with a brush – a fine, flat-tipped reed – and black ink made of gum and lamp black mixed with water; chapter headings were in red ink derived from iron oxide. The writing was usually upon rolls of papyrus fibre or on *ostraka* – sherds of pottery or flakes of stones – or on leather or cloth. Writing on papyrus was one of Egypt's more important legacies; its lightness enabled it to cross frontiers with ease and for more than 4,000 years much of the civilised world wrote on these rolls, of which the export was an important part of Egyptian revenue. "Civilisation, or at least the story of humanity," Pliny the Elder remarked in 70 AD, "rests on papyrus." Our paper and pens today are directly derived from the tools of the Egyptian scribe.

Egypt also invented the earliest illustrated books. Her "Books of the Dead," placed in wealthy tombs from the time of the New Kingdom onwards, were splendidly ornamented with illuminated scenes and patterns. Their presence guaranteed a happy future life, both human and divine.

Egypt may also claim to have invented the strip cartoon, in using pictures with an appropriate written commentary. And may we not regard the international symbols which we use increasingly today, on road signs, tourist guides and publicity brochures, as latter-day descendants of hieroglyphs?

. . . and of a rational division of time

"In the matters of this world," Herodotus informs us, "they (the priests of Heliopolis) told me unanimously that it was the Egyptians who first invented the year by dividing the cycle of the seasons into twelve parts; this they did, say the priests, by observing the stars." Days, months and years were known, in fact, long before the time of the pyramids. According to the most eminent authority in this field, the Egyptian calendar "is certainly the only rational calendar which has ever been devised."

What stars did the ancient Egyptians observe in devising the year of 365 days? The moon certainly – the average length of twenty-five lunar years always gives this number – but more especially Sirius, which appears at the time of the Nile's spate, towards the 19th of July. The Egyptians divided the year into twelve months of equal length, placing five epagomenic, or additional, days at the end. The months were grouped in three sets of four and numbered according to their place in the three seasons: first, second, third or fourth month of the flood, the seedtime and the harvest. Each month was divided into three groups of ten days. There was no leap year, and from this omission it is possible to establish an absolute chronology of pharaonic history (the ancient Egyptians used relative chronology only, starting from the accession of each new sovereign). The calendar fell behind by one day in every four years and, these days accumulating, the new year coincided with the rising of Sirius only once in every 1460 years. This phenomenon occurred in 139 AD which provides a point of departure from which a universal chronology can be established.

To Egypt we owe also the division of the day into twenty-four hours. Although for general purposes the Egyptians used hours of unequal lengths, the twelve hours of daylight and twelve of darkness varying with the time of year, the concept of the "equal hour" was known. By about the fifth century BC the months came to acquire the names of festivals that were celebrated in them. This lucid system appealed to the Ptolemies, who adopted it during the Hellenistic period, adding an intercalary day every four years (Decree of Canopus).

Julius Caesar, wishing to replace his lunar calendar with a solar one, summoned the Alexandrian astronomer Sosigenes, in 46 BC. Sosigenes took the Alexandrian calendar as his basis but suppressed the epagomenic days and created months of an unequal number of days; he retained the names of the ten Roman months, adding those of Julius and Augustus, and made January 1st, the date of Rome's foundation, the first day of the year.

The Julian calendar, in use till 1582, was reformed by Pope Gregory XIII. He suppressed the period from the 4th to the 15th of October 1582, in order to eliminate the discrepancy caused by the fact that the Julian year exceeded the solar year by 11 minutes and 40 seconds.

Pioneers of healing

Our knowledge of Egyptian medicine comes in the main from eight surviving papyri that deal with the subject. The ancient Egyptians believed that illness was caused by evil spirits and could be cured by magic. Recourse to magicians, the common practice especially in rural areas, did not preclude the parallel existence of a true science of medicine. Its treatises cover a very wide field, extending from respiratory infections to bone surgery, from gastrology to toothache, from gynaecology to veterinary science. Descriptions of the diseases are followed by efficacious treatments. The Ebers papyrus contains this interesting statement: "The beginning of the doctor's art: the knowledge of the working and nature of the heart. It contains vessels which go to all the members. Those points which the physician tests with his fingers, whether on the head, the nape of the neck, the hands, the heart itself, the arms, the legs or any other place, all reveal something of the heart, for its vessels go to all parts of the body. This is why it speaks in the vessels of each member." The heart was not only the centre of physical life, it was also the seat of the emotions, the intellect and the will. It had an important religious role, for without it neither life nor after-life were possible; it was for this reason that the heart was left in place when the other internal organs were removed in embalmment. The vessels of the heart carried not only blood but all the body's other liquids: tears, sperm, urine. Curiously enough, although they knew about the pulse, they knew nothing of the kidneys.

Many of the remedies recommended would be acceptable to modern medicine: honey, milk and cream for a sore throat, inhalations for bronchitis, extra nourishment for tuberculosis. Treatments prescribed for the urinary tract prove that bilharziasis (parasitic haematuria), responsible for such ravages today in rural areas, was endemic even in those distant times. Gynaecological problems, including cancer of the womb, contraception, sterility and tests to determine the sex of the foetus are dealt with. Discharges of the ear, inflammations and otitis were treated with pellets for the ear passages, ointments, injections, compresses and fumigation. Dentists could treat inflammation of the gums, drain abscesses and fill teeth; the examination of mummies has shown that fillings were composed of a mineral cement and loose teeth were secured with gold wire. In a land where dust and lack of hygiene cause many diseases of the eyes and eyelids particular attention was paid to them; antimony and other substances were recommended for the treatment of trachoma and cataract; hemeralopia, which causes night blindness, was treated appropriately by a decoction of animal liver; liver extract is used in its control today.

In the field of orthopaedics the ancient Egyptians excelled; all types of fractures, contusion of the vertebrae, dislocation of the jaw, were described and suitable treatment – setting of the bone, massage, bandages – indicated; in very serious cases, such as a lesion of the spinal cord, the physician declared his helplessness: "an injury for which nothing can be done," (Edwin Smith Papyrus).

Doctors were trained in the "House of Life," a learned institution with many functions, but we do not know how they were taught or by whom. Herodotus tells us that the profession was highly specialised: dentists, oculists and stomach specialists were practising in the Old Kingdom. A doctor might specialise in more than one field, or might have a further profession such as that of scribe, veterinary surgeon or priest; he might also have assistants responsible for nursing, bandaging and preparation of prescriptions. Doctors were always paid in kind.

The skill of the Egyptian physicians was renowned throughout Greece and Asia Minor. The Hittite and later the Persian Kings consulted them. Hippocrates and Galen themselves acknowledged that they had acquired a large part of their science from Egyptian works, which they had consulted in Memphis in the temple of Imhotep, patron and later god of medicine. We know from Pliny that the Romans also summoned the greatest doctors of Egypt for consultations. Such a reputation must have rested on solid achievements.

The cradle of wisdom and monotheism

The most immediately striking feature of ancient Egyptian religion is its polytheism: an incredible multiplicity of gods and goddesses in animal form – cow, crocodile, ram, lion, cat, ibis, monkey, bull, hippopotamus, vulture, falcon, to name but a few. For an explanation we must look into prehistory. Long before it became a unified realm the country was occupied by tribes of hunters who had come down from the desert to clear and cultivate the valley. Each tribe had its own god – an animal or a tree – which it continued to cling to after the country's unification. It is important to recognise here one of Egypt's most fundamental and permanent characteristics: her conservatism, which was elevated to the status of dogma, leading her to set new beliefs beside the old without ever suppressing the institutions of the past. Another characteristic habit, going back to very early times, was the uniting of the names and functions of several deities in one god, so that all their divine attributes were assumed by the chief god of the *nome* or province. The gods of the great cities tended to embrace all others; from this arose the idea of a universal deity, impersonal and immanent in each god.

The concept is present in the religious thought of Egypt in all periods. It is enshrined in the "Books of Wisdom" which were taught in the colleges of the scribes. These precious books, as old as the pyramids, traced the "path of life," which led to happiness. They taught the rules of life, of politeness and etiquette, by a system that contrasted the good with the bad. They affirmed that men were "created equal" but were themselves responsible for inequality. Amongst the virtues most valued were humanity, submissiveness, prudence, reserve and also respect for government; all public disturbance inspired horror as a sacrilege. Although these teachings were essentially social they did not exclude a moral and even a metaphysical element:

rectitude, charity to the less fortunate, submission to the will of god. The name of God, without further definition, recurs in all epochs, as the following examples show: "Events do not follow the plans of men but the designs of God" (Ptahotep, Old Kingdom); "God knows the man who serves him" (Merikare, 11th dynasty); "God will glorify the name of his servant" (anon., 18th dynasty); "Man is mud and straw, God is his builder" (Amenhotep, end of New Kingdom); "Happy is he who walks in the way of God" (Petisis, fourth century BC). Such forms of expression are not confined to the "Books of Wisdom"; they occur in many other documents and prove beyond doubt that ancient Egypt had a concept of monotheism, in the shape of a transcendent deity without a name or form. But, faithful to her tradition of religious conservatism, she tried, over a period of thousands of years, to reconcile her religious thought with the legacy of the past.

At one strange and fascinating point in her history Egypt did indeed attempt to free herself from this superfluity of gods. In the fourteenth century BC, at one of the most brilliant periods in Egyptian culture, the philosopher king Amenophis IV broke with the priests of Amon and left Thebes to make his capital at Tell-el-Amarna. Here he instituted a new cult of the sun, anticipating by eighteen hundred years the solar monotheism of Julian the Apostate. He gave the universal god a visible sign, the sun disk, and a name, *Aton*; himself he proclaimed *Akhenaton*, son and image of the god. This one god was creator of all men, Egyptians and foreigners alike, for he saw in the union in one faith of his own people and their subject races an effective tool for cementing his empire. The failure of his religious revolution was due in part to the "subversive" element it introduced in making the divine being a visible god, endowed with a name. By so doing it broke with the past robbing the other gods of their share of the omnipresent divinity.

Yet the idea of one god and the religious spirituality which went with it left a profound imprint. Its effects were embodied in the "House of Life," a college of sages whose meditations led them to a high level of intellectual speculation, and to a very subtle concept of the divine. They envisaged a transcendent god, uncreated and omnipresent, whose nature was unfathomable, who watched over man and protected him, who ruled his destiny and inspired in him a love approaching ecstasy. This sublimated idea was ultimately derived from the idea of divine judgement awaiting the dead beyond the grave, a fundamental concept which had existed from the time of the Old Kingdom. It engendered the notion of responsibility which developed, little by little, into that of conscience, which the sages described as "god in man." From this came an acute sense of sin and of the need for repentance. In its last centuries this religion saw the gap widening further and further between the religious thought of the temples, affirming a transcendent god, and popular belief. Unsatisfied by this remote and abstract god the people attached themselves more and more to his visible forms and earthly symbols.

Land of the Bible

After the expulsion of the Hyksos, the Asiatic invaders who had dominated the Nile valley from the eighteenth to the beginning of the sixteenth centuries, Egypt extended her rule as far as the Euphrates to shield herself from predatory neighbours to the east. This marked the beginning of the "cosmopolitan" period of her history. The ebb and flow of conquest brought not only prisoners, spoil and tributes from other lands, but also their customs and beliefs. It is not surprising that after this period of ferment foreign elements appear in her culture and that of her subject peoples. We find, for example, the same absence of distinction between intellectual and moral rules in the Egyptian theologians and the Biblical prophets. The book of Proverbs has much in common with Egyptian collections of wise sayings; it contains in particular several profound ideas adapted from the Teachings of Amenemhet (first millennium BC). Akhenaton's innovations, his desire to unite men in one faith, cannot have been unknown to Canaanite writers; the *Hymn to the Sun,* written by Akhenaton himself, which in its lyricism and religious intensity is one of the great achievements of world literature, must surely have inspired the psalmist in certain passages of Psalm 104.

One could give many more examples. But let us look at the second book of the Pentateuch, which tells the story of the Jewish exodus from Egypt. Was this episode, which was to have such incalculable results, seen as an important event by the inhabitants of the Nile? On the contrary, it passed completely unnoticed or, at the most, was regarded as the banal departure of one of many Bedouin groups, incited to insubordination by a renegade officer. If the name of Egypt occurs 680 times in the Bible, we have so far discovered only one Egyptian reference to Israel, on a triumphal stele – to which it has given its name – in the funeral temple of Ramses II at Thebes. This dates from the fifth year of his successor Merneptah; of its twenty-eight lines of text, all but three are dedicated to Pharaoh's victory over the Libyans. The others state: "Israel is devastated. Her seed no longer exists."

When did the exodus take place and what route did it follow? The arrival of the Hebrews in Egypt dates from the time of the Hyksos, between the Middle and the New Kingdom; they established themselves in a semi-desert region near the frontier town of Pithom, for which according to the Bible, they were set to making bricks. Biblical chronology and archaeological investigations at Jericho place the departure from Egypt within the 19th dynasty, whose sovereigns decided to subject an Asiatic people to the "Laws of the Palace." One aspect of these events, the persecution of the Jews, undoubtedly took place during the reign of Seti I (1312-1298 BC), second king of the dynasty and father of Ramses II. The Asiatic subject princes of the time lived at the court of Pharaoh, where many held important posts. The social context of the time fits perfectly with what we know of the character of Moses; his Egyptian education and his probable initiation into the teachings of the sages formed an excellent preparation for his future as legislator and prophet. The Egyptian concept of a unique, all-creating god, brought into being by his own will, and whose impenetrable essence would bring death to anyone who sought to look upon it – is this not found in the passage of Exodus where God replies to Moses "Thou canst not see my face: for there shall no man see me and live."

The Bible combines two traditions, dating from antiquity, concerning the route followed by the Jews. According to the more recent they went along the Mediterranean coast past the Egyptian strongholds that marked the imperial route from Pelusium to Gaza; the sea that parted for them was formed of the lagoons to the east of modern Port Said. The second tradition, which seems more authentic, led Moses and his tribe across the isthmus of Suez to the Red Sea.

There remains the New Testament account of the "Flight into Egypt." One of the elements that sustained the faith of the Egyptian early Christians during the persecutions was a sense of pride that their country had been singled out as the refuge of the infant Christ, and that they had seen the accomplishment of the words of the biblical prophets who foretold the turning of Egypt from paganism to God and the worship of Yahwe in Egyptian temples (Isaiah, Chapter XIX, verses 18 onwards).

An influence as great as Egypt herself

Man can be said to survive only through his capacity to organise, to change his environment and to exploit its possibility through technology. The inhabitants of the Nile valley possessed all these qualities to a remarkable degree, making their country a model of organisation, of technical competence and artistic creativity. From antiquity the "Egyptian miracle" has justly enjoyed the highest acclaim.

Secure in her splendid isolation, Egypt developed a characteristically national culture which, it seems, she made no conscious attempt to export. But the trade which she early established with neighbouring countries and the imperial expansion of the second millennium brought her into contact with other peoples. She left on these a strong imprint, bringing them her values and "mysteries." Her influence extended to Africa, the Near East, and throughout the Mediterranean.

Nubia, the gateway to Africa, was exploited for its exotic products, and later colonised by

Egypt. It yielded gold, precious stones, hardwoods, ivory, ebony and livestock. When the New Kingdom extended its rule to the fourth cataract, Nubia was given an autonomous administration and adopted Egyptian beliefs, customs and writing. Through Nubia Egypt had an incontestable influence on black Africa, transmitting, amongst other things, certain metallurgic techniques.

From Asia she imported the timber, copper, silver, iron and semi-precious stone that she lacked. From there also she acquired the olive, the horse, bronze working, and international law, the invention of Mesopotamia. Following the extension of the empire to the Euphrates, political, commercial and matrimonial exchanges multiplied. Holding the monopoly of African products, she exported them to the eastern principalities, sending grain to the Hittites and the Athenians, alum to the oracle at Delphi and gold to the rulers of Asia. Babylonians, Hittites, Assyrians, Lydians and Persians, Phoenicians, Palestinians and Syrians were all influenced by her technical innovations and governmental organisation. Solomon, Pharaoh's son-in-law, undoubtedly took Egyptian administration as his model in giving his Jewish kingdom an effective organisation.

Although, along with Mesopotamia, Egypt invented writing, she did not devise a true alphabet; she possessed signs corresponding to individual consonants which could have been combined to form an alphabet capable of writing all words, but she did not fully explore this possibility. She used other types of signs concurrently and contented herself with furnishing certain Canaanites with the idea of using images to represent sounds, from which our alphabet was perfected.

In the realm of science, the few texts so far discovered dealing with mathematics, medicine or astronomy show a utilitarian bias, describing systems designed to meet specific needs, rather than general laws. The Egyptians could calculate the area of a circle and the volume of a pyramid; they sometimes even show that they are aware of the autonomy of an argument. But it seems that in this sphere they were outclassed by the science of Babylon.

The inimitable style of her art, on the other hand, enjoyed immense prestige; scarabs, bronzes, vases, amulets were imported, copied and exported again throughout the Mediterranean world. Egyptianising motifs are found in the art of Phoenicia, Syria, Assyria and Persia.

Egypt also excelled in the field of literature, a genuine literature of extreme richness; all genres are represented in it: apothegms, short stories, novels, satire, love poetry, hymns, biography, epitaphs. Literary themes and style are centred on man and the problems of this life, and show the Egyptian through his joys and sufferings, hopes and fears. The stories of marvels or anecdotal tales, the first of their kind, the splendid histories and tales of adventure that Egypt launched upon the world have enjoyed a marvellous success, being retold and imitated to the present day.

One must, in conclusion, mention the prestige of her religious thought and her moral code, which were propagated throughout the Near East. The Hittite prayers to the sun echo the hymns that were addressed to Aton; the fame of this solar monotheism was such that the Hittite kings caused themselves to be addressed as "My Sun." A prince of the Phoenician city of Byblos wrote in the eleventh century BC: "It is from Egypt that wisdom first came to my country."

10

11

12

9. A felucca, the typical lateen-rigged boat used in Egypt, on the Nile near Aswan.

10. Pharaonic inscription on a stone in the Nile near Aswan.

11. Writing was invented in Egypt, almost at the same time as in Mesopotamia, but quite independently.

12. Older people wear black, in contrast to the brightly coloured headdresses of the young.

13. A shop selling wheat flour in Orgada, on the Red Sea.

13

14

15

16

17

14-15. Desert landscapes in the delta area near Alexandria. The brusque changes from fertile to arid land are typical of this zone.

16. This elaborate construction is actually a dovecote.

17. Blue eyes or fair skin are vestiges of the many invasions Egypt has suffered.

18. Feluccas on the Nile at Abu Korkas near Beni Hassan.

19

20

21

19. Village scene on Elephantine Island, together with Philae the most famous of the Lake Nasser islands.

20-21. Nubian villages. Nubia, bordering on the Sudan, is the southernmost part of Egypt and is in many ways a link between the Mediterranean and black Africa.

22. The village of El Dyaba, near the tombs of Beni Hassan.

23

23. The monastery of Saint Anthony. In the mountains behind the monastery, at the top of steps carved in the stone by the monks, is the cave where Saint Anthony retired in hermitage. It can be visited, and on certain occasions masses are held there.

24. The desert of Tih in central Sinai.

25. Typical house in El Chattara, north of Aswan. Vaulted roofs have been used since pharaonic times.

24

25

26

27

28

26-28. Even the simplest houses tend to be painted bright colours. One of the most common occasions for decorating the façades of houses is for the celebration held when a member of the family returns from pilgrimage to Mecca.

29

29. The Bedouins live on the edge of the desert and their traditional costumes are most distinctive, especially the sequin-decorated or embroidered veils of the married women.

30

30. The desert of central Sinai, at the foot of Mount Saint Catherine.

31. Desert landscape near El Mazar.

32. A Muslim cemetery in the Sinai desert.

31

32

33

34

35

36

33. A well in the desert.

34. This brave palm tree is indicative of the tenacity of the desert's inhabitants.

35. The road to the oasis of El Kharga.

36. Bedouin women in the desert of northern Sinai.

37. Scarecrow.

38

39

40

38. Making bread in a Nubian village near Aswan. Before it is baked, the bread is placed in the sun to leaven.

39. A funeral in Fayyum.

40. The cemetery of Asyut. Traditional rites at funerals and the way the dead are cared for throughout Egypt reflect ceremonies which go back to long before Islam or Christianity. The presence of weeping women, dressed in blue, at a funeral recalls the bas-reliefs at Sakkara or the paintings at the tomb of Ramosé at Thebes.

41. Irrigation canals near Port Said on the Suez Canal.

42. The houses of the fellahs are built by the fellahs themselves; they are made of sun-baked bricks covered in mud and consist of two or three rooms, one with an oven on which the whole family sleeps in winter.

41

43

43. *The Post Office at Aswan.*

44. *The city-centre and market-place at Aswan.*

45. *Schoolchildren in Qena.*

44

45

46. A painting of the vulture goddess Mut in the tomb of Tausert, in the Valley of the Kings.

48

47

47-48. The motifs of ancient Egyptian painting are often repeated in modern tapestries and rugs. The Ramsès Wissa Wassef art school encourages young people in this art (47), often producing remarkable results (48).

Pharaonic Egypt

THE SOURCES OF HISTORY (c. 10,000-6,000 BC)

A heterogeneous population

Egypt was settled relatively late – at the beginning of the Neolithic period – by various distinct groups that apparently originated from the ancient nomads of northern Africa. These were hunters, who roamed the game-filled forests and grasslands which covered this region; they drove before them huge herds of long-horned cattle, such as we find engraved on the rocks of the Egyptian desert. These peoples seem to have been basically Nilotic and African, with a Hamito-Semitic admixture.

As the savannah of the Sahara became progressively drier, the tribes withdrew to moister areas: oases, inland lakes and small tributaries of the Nile. When these dried up they were forced to settle on patches of higher ground along the edge of the Nile valley. The Nile at that time was a devastating torrent which spent itself in a marshland of reeds and papyrus. This was the home of all manner of wildlife: hippopotamus, crocodiles, lions, hyena, jackals, cheetah, gazelles, wild oxen, reptiles and scorpions. At the floodtime all these fled to the desert. The need to clear these marshy thickets and to control the annual inundation of the Nile forced the nomads to a more settled way of life; to their traditional pursuits of hunting and fishing they added agriculture. The native flora was poor; it comprised only marsh vegetation, date and doum palms, sycamore, willow, tamarisk and olive. New species were later introduced from abroad. The fauna was gradually enriched by importations of cattle, donkeys, sheep and goats from Africa and Asia. The horse did not appear until the coming of the Hyksos at the end of the eighteenth century BC and was used only to draw chariots.

The first industries

The change from hunting to an agricultural way of life led to the development of certain specialised crafts, particularly the manufacture of tools and weapons of flint and polished stone. Bone provided pointed implements and punches or needles for stitching skins. The Neolithic period saw the invention of the weaving of cloth and basketry. A red or black ceramic was produced in a variety of forms – plates, bowls, jugs, etc.; handles appeared on large vessels. In the Eneolithic phase, during which both flint and metal – gold or copper – were used in tool making, the flint industry techniques improved. Weaving methods developed, but the greatest achievements were in ceramics, which showed a great variety of form and abundant decoration; the characteristic blue or green enamel of Egyptian faïence was developed. The decorated pottery of the end of this period is of a quality unequalled in later eras. Small quantities of glassware were produced for the first time. Superb vases in hard stone were also made.

The final age of Egyptian pre-history, from about 3600 BC, contained three periods. The first was the Early Predynastic Period of Amratian culture, in which the use of flint predominated and elegantly shaped vases in limestone, alabaster, basalt and granite, and statuettes of bone and ivory, were made. The second was the Middle Predynastic Period of Gerzean culture (c. 3300) in which building in mud (sun-baked) brick was introduced and in which amulets, tools and weapons of copper, decorated ceramics and hard-stone vases appear. The third was the Late Predynastic Period (c. 3200 BC), which saw the dawn of sculpture with statuettes of animals and naked women; the decorative techniques already show the basic conventions of pharaonic bas-relief.

An embryo administration

Egypt's political organisation developed from the independent communities which, centred around the shrine of a god and ruled by a priest-king, grew up along the banks of the Nile. The absorption of some of these states by their more powerful neighbours led to a regrouping into two large administrative divisions: Upper and Lower Egypt. The original units were preserved into historic times in the form of "nomes" or provinces, each possessing its own administration and dependent only on the centralising services of the pharaoh. The most important township formed the capital of the nome, and was the seat not only of local government but of the local god, "Lord of the town and of the nome."

The two rulers of Upper and Lower Egypt were equally the representatives of Horus. The frontier between the kingdoms lay a little to the south of the ancient city of Memphis. The traditions and ways of life of the two regions were different; the north, more fertile and, from her position, more open to foreign influence, evolved more rapidly than the south, on whom she imposed her dominance and by the side of whose gods she placed her own.

In the Eneolithic period the Egyptians undertook the enormous enterprise of levelling the Nile valley and of controlling the flood by a system of canals and dykes. On so fertile a soil this quickly brought a prosperity which passed subsistence level, and opened the way for a true civilisation. In the towns of the eastern delta, the elements of a system of writing were already in existence.

Local gods and creation myths

The beliefs of the ancient Egyptians were rooted in prehistory, in the local gods surviving from the early fragmentation of the country. Many of these primitive divinities appeared in the Egyptian pantheon sometimes changing their names or natures according to later religious re-alignments. Stories explaining the nature of the universe also evolved in prehistory. The chief gods included the Ocean – the primordial water, origin of all things; the sky, personified by the goddess Nut; the sun god Re, who crossed the sky in two boats of the day and night, to be swallowed at nightfall by the goddess Nut, in whose body he travelled through the night to be born anew next morning; the moon, sometimes represented by Thoth, sometimes by Khons; the stars, especially Sothis, whose rising marked the coming of the flood and the start of the new year; the earth god Geb, husband of Nut; the air, Shu, who sundered the embrace of Nut and Geb by force. The demi-gods of the primitive religions lived on in the hearts of the people: Hapi (the Nile), Satet (the fertile countryside), Nepri (the grain god), Ernemutet (goddess of the harvest), Thoneris (the hippopotamus goddess, protectress of pregnant women), and many others.

The animal cults also go back to prehistory, deriving from the belief that certain animals housed one of the souls of a divinity. The most famous were the bulls of Apis, an incarnation of Ptah of Memphis; the ram of Amon at Thebes, and of Khnum at Elephantine; the goat of Osiris at Busiris; the crocodile of Sebek at Fayyum; the cat of Bastis at Bubastis. These ancient cults were never abolished, though sacred animals were later removed from temples. As alliances united the cities each god acquired a wife and child; these triads constitute the most ancient attempts at a hierarchy of gods, which in their turn were grouped and regrouped with the progressive unification of the country to form huge pantheons.

Despite the lengthy and elaborate speculations of later theologians of ancient Egypt, we possess no sacred book which codified their beliefs. This is explained by the fact that the basis of religion was the cult, especially the local cult. This was a state institution subject only to pharaoh; the diversity of its traditions precluded any unification of dogma. Dogmas varied from place to place and even from person to person. The educated belief in a monotheistic divinity, expressed in the Books of Wisdom, also may have derived from prehistory. That era never ceased to influence the religious thinking of the temples.

Objects found in the graves, such as food placed near the bodies, toilet objects and tools, attest to a belief in an after-life. The turning of the heads of the dead towards their dwelling huts suggests that it was believed that they wished still to watch their earthly home and descendants. The continued association of the spirit with the body required the preservation of the latter intact, its burial in the desert away from the damp and its nourishment. This was the origin of the funeral feasts held near the dead and the offerings of bread and water made daily at the shrine attached to each tomb.

THE THINITE KINGDOM (c. 3000-2778 BC)

Unity and divinity

In all fields the Thinite period was one of gestation, in which various elements came together, were co-ordinated and achieved perfection. The first two dynasties have in embryo all the future grandeur of Egypt. The sovereigns of the two realms, of which the capitals were Buto in the north and Hierakonpolis in the south, were known in historic times as "Servants of Horus." According to the rare records that have come down to us, an attempt to unite the kingdoms seems to have been made by a king whom modern historians have called Scorpion (from the hieroglyph which represents his name). Despite the fact that this attempt was crowned by a victory, the two kingdoms seem to have remained substantially intact. His probable successor, King Narmer, achieved the unification attempted by his predecessor. His exploits are depicted on the two faces of a votive palette in green schist found at Hierakonpolis; on a mace-head found in the same place the king is shown wearing the double crown, the red of Lower Egypt and the white of Upper Egypt. Was Narmer the first king of all Egypt rather than (as tradition asserts) King Menes? Or are they perhaps the same person?

To secure his position as ruler of all Egypt, Menes founded a new capital where the two kingdoms met; this became the city of Memphis.

It is difficult to reconstruct the history of the early reigns. Manetho, high priest of Heliopolis in the time of Ptolemy I, has left a chronology of the pharaohs. He divided the first rulers into two dynasties called "Thinite" from their place of origin, the town of This, the capital of the eighth nome of Upper Egypt, which was somewhere near Abydos. The earliest records we have suggest that these kings founded the political and administrative system that supported the grandeur of the Egyptian monarchy. They had to protect their new realm both from enemies without and dissidents within.

A divine monarchy

The Thinite kings were absolute monarchs whose authority was divine. The king was the incarnation of Horus, the ancient falcon god, conqueror of the country. The royal title was "He of the two lands." Nekhbet, the vulture goddess of the north, and Wadjet, the cobra goddess of the south, were his protectresses. Thus his de facto power was sanctioned by divine right. Soon afterwards a third dignity was added to the royal titulary, the double emblem of Upper Egypt (the reed) and Lower Egypt (the bee). Precedence was given to the goddess and to the emblem of the south, by virtue of its victory over the north.

The need to bind together the two former kingdoms gave rise to a ceremony that persisted throughout pharaonic history: the royal enthronement or coronation. The fourfold ceremony consisted of putting on the white crown of Upper Egypt and the red crown of Lower Egypt, the uniting of the double country by interweaving of symbolistic plants, and the tour of the wall (the white wall built to protect the south from invasion from the delta).

Another traditional ceremony was the Sed festival. Its exact significance is uncertain, but it seems to derive from the primitive rite of deposing and perhaps killing the king when his allotted time came to an end. This festival was a ritualised compromise: the king, in place of deposition, renewed his lease of power and began a new reign with rejuvenated strength. The Sed festival became a kind of jubilee that reaffirmed the rule of the king, and was held at the sovereign's discretion.

The shaping of government

Very little is known of the details of Thinite government. The king, ruling through a hierarchy of central and provincial officials, probably presided himself over the various "Houses" or ministries; the office of vizier does not seem to have yet existed. Documents recording annual events were lodged in the royal archive.

Even less is known of provincial government. The development of agriculture and irrigation implies the existence of officials responsible for overseeing the waterways. This was probably the origin of the office of "nomarch" of which the functions were to improve the yield of the land, to make a biennial census of the population, and to record the height of the Nile flood so that prospects for the crops could be assessed. Each nome was the seat of a judicial tribunal; this suggests the existence of civil law.

Apogee of the use of hard stones

The funerary architecture of the period developed from the prehistoric tomb. The oblong hole of the latter became a rectangular chamber faced with brick and surrounded by small rooms for the reception of offerings. Its entrance, to the east, was marked by two stelae. Stone was not used until the end of the 2nd dynasty.

The Thinite artists excelled in schist and steatite sculpture and in the carving of stelae and ivory placques. The rare surviving animal reliefs (lions and monkeys) show a remarkable perfection and elegance. Their statues vary in quality; some pieces are primitive, others are of a quality which anticipate the best of later productions. The earliest royal statues are two dating from the end of the 2nd dynasty. But it is in the working of flint, alabaster and other hard stones that Thinite technique reached its apogee: elegance of form, quality of finish, and a happy exploitation of the markings of the stone. The Thinite vases, in granite, diorite, rock crystal, green schist and alabaster, have never been surpassed; they are marvels of technical perfection and refinement.

The restructuring of the pantheon

The union of the two previously autonomous kingdoms made necessary a reordering of the official hierarchy of the gods. This was effected by making Horus, the dynastic god of the conquering king, supreme over all the other gods of the country, both north and south. This re-adjustment was disturbed by a king of the 2nd dynasty, who declared himself the incarnation of Seth, the enemy of Horus. Although this decision, which caused grave disorders, was without permanent consequences, it left the Egyptians perpetually on their guard against this hated god, the incarnation of evil.

It was at this time that the solar mythology of Heliopolis was evolved. According to this Nu, the primordial water, had existed since the beginning of time; from it Atum, the sun, created himself; he then engendered Shu and Tefnut (air and moisture), who in their turn gave birth to Geb, the earth god, and Nut the sky goddess. Nut was the mother of Osiris, Seth, Isis and Nephthys, the protagonists of the famous legend of Osiris; these nine gods formed the great Ennead, the lesser Ennead being composed of Horus and secondary gods.

The legend of Osiris had a strong hold over the imaginations of the people. As the oldest son of Geb and Nut, he inherited the earth and ruled it benificently. His brother Seth, jealous of his power, captured him by guile, killed him and threw his body into the waves. Isis and Nephthys, searching for him, found his defiled and decomposing body in Egypt. According to the Pyramid Texts, Osiris, purified and remade, came back to life and engendered the infant Horus, whom his mother Isis brought up in the swamps. The death of Osiris, however, put an end to his rule on earth, and his realm was henceforth that of the other world.

The variety of mythologies that continued to flourish proves that, though politically united, the country was far from having any unity of religious thought. This diversity suggests fierce struggles for ascendancy. In the theology of Hermopolis the supreme god was Thoth, the moon god, an ibis or baboon, the originator of all things. He engendered himself out of chaos and created four pairs of gods (of night, darkness, mystery and eternity). These were charged with preparing the birth of the sun, who triumphed over hostile forces and created the world.

Other cosmogonies evolved, based on that of Heliopolis or Hermopolis, or a mixture of the two. The cosmogony of Memphis honoured Ptah, god of that city. When Memphis became the capital of a unified Egypt, Ptah was promoted to the head of the pantheon; in creating himself he also created eight divinities constituent of himself; these were the great gods of Egypt who formed, with Ptah, an Ennead: Atum his thought, Horus his heart, Thoth his tongue, etc.

In the land of the west beyond the grave – a paradise personified by the beautiful goddess Amentet – Osiris received his faithful. Having undergone the same rites as himself they became his subjects for eternity.

From this time onward, food and possessions buried with the dead testify to the Egyptian belief that the soul of the dead dwelt near the body in the earth, to preserve the body uncorrupted, which was essential for the soul's survival; provisions were stored in neighbouring rooms. The superstructure of the tomb (a rectangular mass of rubble faced with mud brick) gave the dead access to the world of the living. A chimney, later a shaft, communicated with the burial chamber, its upper orifice opening behind the offering niche. By this means the soul could "come out to the day," could return, that is, to this world; by this route also the offerings could magically reach the dead within his tomb.

THE OLD KINGDOM: EGYPT IN HER YOUTH (c. 2778-2263 BC)

The builders of the pyramids

The Old Kingdom spans the histories of the 3rd, 4th, 5th and 6th dynasties. This period saw the birth, maturity and decline of a prodigious empire, of which the capital city was Memphis.

The early history of the 3rd dynasty (c. 2778-2723 BC) is obscure; the order in which its rulers succeeded is uncertain. The second king, the celebrated Djoser, gave a great impetus to the country's development. He was assisted by his chancellor Imhotep, a man of outstanding genius – architect, man of letters and physician – who was also high priest of Heliopolis. The Greeks called him Imouthes and recognised in him Aesculapius, their god of medicine; he was regarded as a sage throughout antiquity and was deified in 525 BC. Manetho wrote of him: "Because of his medical knowledge the Egyptians regard him as Aesculapius. He invented the art of building with cut stone, and dedicated himself to letters." The magnificent architectural complex at Sakkara bears witness to his genius today.

For reasons little understood Djoser transferred his capital from Abydos to Memphis. Here at Sakkara, facing the royal palace of brick and timber, Imhotep built for his sovereign an eternal residence of shining limestone. This is the Step Pyramid, one of the marvels of Egypt and the oldest architecture in stone of which we have knowledge.

Little is known of the reign of Djoser; according to inscriptions and stelae he sent a mining expedition to Sinai and annexed upper Nubia. His probable successor, Sekhemkhet, began a pyramid which was not completed.

Snefru, founder of the 4th dynasty (c. 2723-2563 BC) was famous as a builder and for his military and economic achievements. He brought copper and turquoise from Sinai, and in campaigns in Libya and Nubia he captured many thousands of men and beasts. Three pyramids, built to the north and south of Memphis, and including the first true pyramid, attest his might and glory.

We know almost nothing of the builders of the three great pyramids of Giza – Khufu (Cheops), son of Snefru, Khufre (Khephren) and Menkaure – save their names and their colossal tombs. Their political achievements are lost. Herodotus tells various scandalous stories of them which are quite without foundation. All that can be said is that their reigns are illuminated by the perfection of their art and the grandeur of their monuments.

The early history of the 5th dynasty is unclear. During this period the cult of the sun god Re, centred on Heliopolis, became generally established. The sovereigns linked this state religion with pharaonic authority and prefaced their names with the epithet "Son of Re." Beside their pyramids at Abusir they built strange sun temples of unique design, intended to perpetuate the cult of Heliopolis. Few historical events can be attributed to this dynasty apart from victorious expeditions into Libya and Asia.

The transition from the 5th to the 6th dynasty (c. 2423-2263 BC) seems to have taken place, without violence, under King Teti. Nothing is known of him except that he built a pyramid, on the inner chamber walls of which were engraved the famous "Pyramid Texts." Pepi I, a ruler of ability and a great builder, consolidated the power of the 6th dynasty. He re-established and strengthened the Egyptian rights over the copper mines of Sinai. But by marrying the daughter of a private citizen of Abydos he introduced an element of discord, which caused the disintegration of the political structure of his predecessors.

His eldest son Menenre sent several expeditions to Nubia and extended the power of Egypt. Pepi II, his successor, reigned for ninety-four years, the longest reign in Egyptian annals and perhaps in all history.

Pepi's weak rule grew weaker with age, encouraging the development of a provincial feudalism which seriously infringed and finally usurped royal authority. Encouraged by this internal anarchy, Egypt's turbulent neighbours attacked her frontiers. Very few documents survive from this troubled period.

Sons and heirs of the sun god

Under the Old Kingdom the prestige of the pharaoh reached its apogee. Through the official adoption of the sun cult the pharaohs became sons and heirs of the sun. Their dynastic god, Horus the falcon, was identified with the supreme god of the pantheon, Atum. Djoser introduced the expression "golden sun" into royal protocol; this was changed in the 4th dynasty to "golden Horus" to make it consistent with the other "Horian" titles of the sovereign; it later became "Horus, vanquisher of Seth."

From the beginning of the reign of Snefru the king's personal names, preceded by the title "Son of Re," came to be surrounded by an elliptical cartouche thought to represent the course of the sun about the universe; within this course everything belonged to the king and to his father Re.

The sun cult gradually assimilated the local mythologies. It failed only in the case of Ptah of Memphis, whose priests were too powerful, and of Osiris, whose legend was too much a part of popular culture to be absorbed. The Pyramid Texts of the late 5th dynasty show a dichotomy of religious views. These collections of diconnected sayings contain two strands of thought: one doctrinaire, inspired by the sun god Re; one popular, attached to the legend of Osiris, god of death. The two currents later united, but their relationship remains difficult to interpret.

How was the soul of pharaoh transported to the next world to dwell with the sun? According to the Pyramid Texts this was achieved through magic formulae which assured the king eternal life, among his brother gods, in the service of Re.

This faith in the royal journey to the sun, which was set beside the old beliefs in Osiris, was responsible in time for the development of a new religious idea. The sun destiny, originally reserved for the sovereign alone, was gradually extended by them to the family, then to the officials whose company was judged agreeable in after-life. It was obtained by the concession of a tomb in the precincts of the royal necropolis.

Traditions surviving from the old Osiris cult required that in order to unite with the sun the king must undergo a judgement similar to that which Horus underwent at Heliopolis. He must be judged to have administered on earth the justice of Re. The same obligation was exacted from all to whom the privilege of the sun had been granted.

With the crumbling of royal authority all privileges, including the privilege of the sun, became so widely diffused as to become common right. The rulers of the Middle Kingdom did not think it useful to reclaim the privilege; the usurpation became accepted.

The rulers of the Old Kingdom do not seem to have pursued an expansionist foreign policy; the Asian campaigns were defensive only. Egypt's chief aim was to colonise Nubia; under Pepi II the Nubians, no doubt exploited and maltreated, revolted, and skirmishes occurred. Inscriptions of the period suggest a great increase in foreign trade; wood for building construction was imported from Byblos, incense and semi-precious stones from the Land of Punt.

A strongly centralised administration

At the beginning of the 4th dynasty, before the number of central and provincial officials had grown excessively, King Snefru instituted the office of vizier. This chief executive was responsible for the treasury, the judiciary, for agriculture and for the archive office. In the last important documents were kept: royal decrees, title deeds, contracts and wills. The Treasury consisted originally of two Houses, the white (Upper Egypt) and the red (Lower Egypt); these were united to form "the Double White House." The Treasury was responsible for collecting all the produce owed by the country to the "great House" – the palace – and for storing it in the "double Storehouse." As chief justice the vizier presided over the "six great Houses," the state audience chambers. As minister of agriculture he directed one of the most important government services. There were two agricultural departments, one dealing with livestock, the other with crops. On the edge of the desert lay land insufficiently flooded for regular cultivation; this was royal property and used as pasture and for kitchen gardens.

"Chiefs of missions" were responsible for transmitting their vizier's orders and for relaying to him reports from the provinces. They were assisted by head administrators, by deputy heads, by subsidiary officers and by an army of scribes. The profession of scribe was much esteemed for the knowledge and prestige it brought with it.

The "nomarchs," or heads of the provincial administrative districts, had wide powers. Originally merely prefects, who could expect to be transferred more than once in their careers, they tended in time to become established in their posts. They enriched themselves, achieved virtual independence and their offices became hereditary. In this way a landed aristocracy gradually developed, independent of the crown and reluctant to render dues. Robbed of their authority by this feudalism, which its weakness had not been able to prevent, the 6th dynasty collapsed, following the long and indulgent reign of Pepi II.

Officials originally received food and maintenance in exchange for services, the most capable succeeding to the most important posts. But very soon the king began rewarding his favourites with various gifts in the form of funeral donations: sarcophagi, stelae, offering tables. He next gave them grants of land, of which the revenue was intended to maintain the funerary cult. Similar grants were made to priests for the upkeep of their temples. This dispersal of the sovereign's land encouraged decentralisation and brought about the impoverishment and eventual decline of the monarchy of Memphis.

An architecture for eternity

Egypt created two architectural forms in the service of the dead: the pyramid for kings, the mastaba for subjects. Royal tombs only assumed a magnificence to match the god-like status of the monarch with the beginning of the 3rd dynasty, when stone began to be used. Then the brick superstructures gave way to huge bench-like mounds with slightly inclined vertical faces of stone. These were called mastabas (from the Arab "bench"). On the east face of the mound was a great rectangular stele in the form of a closed door, known as the "false door stele," carved with the names and titles of the dead. Before it stood a table for offerings.

Six mastabas were built for the necropolis of King Djoser at Sakkara. They form the approach to what was to become the characteristic funeral monument of the kings of the Old and Middle Kingdoms: the pyramids. Its huge tiers symbolised the stairway by which the king ascended to the sun. From one of the courts of the north temple a long ramp led, through an enormous portal, to the funeral shaft, which gave access to the burial chamber, entirely lined with granite. Cross passages led to storerooms and funerary apartments; four rooms are decorated with blue-glazed tiles.

Within the great enclosure wall attendant buildings were disposed. These comprised the mortuary temple of the king to the north, a great courtyard surrounded by chapels, a series of apartments, two "houses" symbolising sovereignty over south and north, and many storerooms. The architecture throughout is distinguished by a great variety of columns, fluted and fascicular, with capitals of stylised plants.

Three pyramids were erected by Snefru. The oldest, the step pyramid at Medum, had an outer covering which is today almost entirely lost. The Bent Pyramid of Dahshur, whose sides present a double gradient, has two descending passages and two burial chambers. The third, to the north of Dahshur, is the first to display the regularity of the perfect pyramid: square in plan, with four faces in the form of isosceles triangles converging at the summit, covered with a revetment of fine smooth limestone.

This is the form adopted by the mighty creations of the 4th dynasty on the Giza plateau, the most famous of the seventy-five pyramids so far recorded. They are symbols of the sun. "Cheops dwells on the horizon," "Great is Khephren," "Divine Menkaure"; these were the names which their founders gave these majestic monuments. They differ from their immediate predecessors in size, in the cut of their masonry blocks and in the granite revetment at the base of the pyramid of Menkaure; the funerary chambers, instead of being below ground, are at the centre of the mass of masonry. A complicated system of ascending and descending corridors leads to the burial chamber, access to which is guarded by a succession of portcullises of a single piece of stone. The blocks were hewn from local quarries and hauled in stages into position on the successive courses of masonry; dressing of the surface began at the top.

An essential part of the funeral complex was the mortuary temple, placed eastwards of the pyramid. Its sanctuary was a version of the early false door; a long covered causeway led down to a reception temple in the valley. The best preserved mortuary temple is the Valley Temple of Khephren. To its north stands the Sphinx of Giza, whose head is a portrait of this pharaoh. This is, rightly, one of the most celebrated monuments of the pharaohs.

Although no temples proper have survived from this remote period, the evolution of temple architecture is traditionally attributed to the Old Kingdom. In its general disposition the type was little altered. The Egyptian temple was seen as the personal residence of the god, not as a place of assembly; it was open to a few initiates only. The temple precinct was surrounded by thick walls of dried brick, entered by pylons or gates fortified by towers. Within the enclosure were gardens and a sacred lake, workrooms, storerooms and accommodation for the priests and workers. The temple itself was built of stone, the material of eternity. A court surrounded by a colonnade led, by an incline, to a gallery with posts or columns. This occupied the width of the court; at its centre a door opened into a pillared chamber known as the Hypostyle Hall; this led to a vestibule which preceded the sanctuary wherein stood the figure of the god, enclosed in a tabernacle, or "naos." Narrow and completely dark, the sanctuary was flanked by the chapels of associated gods. As son of all the gods the king was the only pontiff; however, he delegated the performance of the sacred rites to priests who served in his place. These were divided into groups each of which served the cult for a month. The rites, performed several times a day consisted of the preparation of the god (his bath, anointment, vestment and adorning) and oblatory meals of bread, meats, fruit and drink, which afterwards supplied the needs of the temple attendants. When the ceremonies were concluded the god was undressed, purified and anointed; the priest then closed the doors of the naos and set his seal upon them. He then withdrew, backwards.

In contrast to this tradition the sun temples of the 5th dynasty were open sanctuaries. Within an open court a great podium shaped like a truncated pyramid was surmounted by an obelisk, symbol of the sun, and built of limestone blocks; before it stood the sacrificial altar. The adjacent precinct, with a gateway to the east, contained ancillary buildings, storerooms, lodgings for the priests and sacrificial courts.

The apogee of the creative arts

Around each pyramid were lesser ones, which housed the closest relations of the king. More distant members of his entourage were grouped around him also, as in life. Their tombs were disposed regularly in the form of a city. In early times the tombs consisted of an underground chamber surmounted by a mastaba, with a false-door stele and a little chapel to the east. In time the stele was incorporated in the superstructure; this grew in size and mortuary chambers in increasing numbers were included. The walls of the later chambers were decorated with bas-reliefs or paintings representing a multiplicity of scenes; these provide invaluable information about the daily life of the upper class. Almost entirely enclosed in the south wall of the chapel, and communicating with it only through a narrow slit at eye level, was a special chamber which housed a reserve of statues; it is known as a "serdab." The Old Kingdom was a period of prodigious artistic invention and creativity, particularly in bas-relief and statuary. To assure no want in the after-life the mastaba decorations show a superfluity of pleasures: banquets, music, hunting, fishing ... painted in simple colours according to well-defined conventions. The bas-reliefs of the 5th dynasty show the art to perfection, with a liveliness of detail, harmonious colour and refined execution. Painting on plaster also became an independent art form, producing masterpieces like the celebrated frieze of geese from Medum (beginning of the 4th dynasty; now in Cairo Museum). The importance of statuary is attested by the number of statues found in the funerary chapels of the pyramids and mastabas, some serving the cult, some reserved in the serdabs. These are usually single figures showing the dead person seated, with his hands resting on his thighs, or standing with one leg slightly advanced – or even cross-legged in the attitude of a scribe. Sometimes a family group is represented, the husband and wife standing or sitting, the wife passing her arm affectionately around her husband's shoulder, with one or two children at their side.

The statues constituted "living images" – replacement bodies made of the most durable materials, sometimes wood, but usually limestone, schist, ivory, diorite, granite, alabaster and even copper. It was essential that they should resemble their originals, in order that the soul might recognise and enter its living image; it was also essential that they should be purged of all fault, idealised. The greater of the Egyptian sculptors perfectly reconciled these conflicting ends; the remarkable portraits they have left us show a command of volume, a subtlety of form and modelling, an equilibrium between the human and the divine, that together are embodied in these masterpieces. Though the gods, often shown with the features of the reigning monarch, are solemnly presented, private persons are rendered with some liveliness and expression. The statues are almost always polychrome, red ochre being used for men, yellow ochre for women; the eyes were encrusted to give a life-like impression. Especially memorable are the portraits of Djoser, of Snefru and, especially, of Khephren; the three-figure group of Menkaure; the seated scribes at Cairo and Paris; and the group of Rehotep and Nofret.

Egyptian artists could sometimes relax their rigorous rules and effectively portray physical idiosyncracies – dwarfs and hunchbacks, the old and the obese.

The 4th dynasty was outstanding for its creativity in all the plastic arts. The 5th dynasty is characterised by a delicacy of form and a greater individualisation in portraiture. The 6th dynasty, while retaining command of technique (witness the Pepi in copper at Cairo Museum), betrays an impoverishment of inspiration which prefigures the decadence to follow.

We possess few examples of the minor arts of this period. Those that survive prove that in this sphere also the Egyptians excelled; the gold falcon's head from Hierakonpolis (in Cairo Museum) shows that the goldsmith yielded nothing to other artists.

THE FIRST INTERMEDIARY PERIOD (c. 2263-2160 BC)

A flock without a shepherd

This period extended from the end of the hegemony of Memphis to the beginning of the 11th dynasty.

Civil wars and invasion troubled the country at the end of the 6th dynasty. The Bedouins, who had been heavily defeated by Pepi I, again overran the delta during the feeble reign of Pepi II. In Upper Egypt the nomarchs ran their territories like so many little kingdoms. The common people revolted, dispossessing the nobles and spreading terror in their wake. The fields were no longer cultivated; famine and epidemics increased the disorder. The disturbances seem, however, to have been limited to Memphis and Middle Egypt.

Of the 7th and 8th dynasties (c. 2263-2220 BC) little is known. The former, to which Manetho allots 70 kings and 70 days – symbol of extreme confusion – seems not to have existed. The latter, according to the same authority, counted 27 kings who ruled at Memphis, but the absence of any monument to them testifies to their depleted power.

In about 2220 Kheti, the head of the nome of Heracleopolis, at the entrance to the Fayyum valley, proclaimed himself king of Upper and Lower Egypt. He reigned in fact over Middle Egypt, the north being in the hands of Asiatic invaders and the south under the domination of the nomarchs of Thebes. In about 2130, one of the latter proclaimed himself king under the name of Intef I. Two simultaneous dynasties then divided the country, the 9th and the 10th Heracleopolitan dynasties and the 10th Theban dynasty. They produced two great sovereigns. One was Kheti II of Heracleopolis, known for the *Instructions* he compiled for his son Merikare – a mixture of elevated thoughts and shrewd political comments. He expelled the foreigners from the delta and reorganised its administration, linking the chief towns by canals and consolidating the eastern frontier. The other was Intef II of Thebes, master of a vast territory, who in 2090 took the initiative against the north and occupied the Thinite nome. After a period of struggle the Heracleopolitan dynasty was finally defeated and by about 2050 BC had ceased to exist.

The eclipse of the royal power of Memphis and the existence of several rulers at one time must have degraded the idea of monarchy and divine law. It also brought about a resurgence of local gods and of the cult of Osiris; the latter acquired a growing importance in Heracleopolitan theology, itself the heir of that of Heliopolis. In the south a divinity appeared who was destined to have a brilliant career – Amon.

An art taken over by the populace

During this period the royal necropolis lost its importance. The mastaba was still in use at Memphis but elsewhere the rock tomb was adopted. Here a vertical shaft leads to a funeral chamber, in which sarcophagi and offerings were placed. In the nomes the scenes which decorate the walls are in a more amorphous style, with elongated figures and no overall design; there is less attention to detail but animals are still depicted with skill. The more detailed biographical inscriptions supply important historical evidence.

The double wooden sarcophagi of these tombs are inscribed with texts transitional in character between the Pyramid Texts and the Book of the Dead. On the left side of the sarcophagus two painted eyes allowed the dead person to see what was happening outside, and a large door enabled him to go in and out at will. The sarcophagi are covered in hieroglyphics, usually in blue. On the inside, objects of daily use are represented with a precision which makes them an invaluable source of information, as well as being minor works of art.

Sculpture made no progress; production became standardised. Vessels in alabaster and hard stone were replaced by terracotta. The limestone figurines of servants found at the end of the Old Kingdom gave place to small wooden figures showing naive scenes of common life. One sees the harvest, the counting of cattle, the making of bread and ale, women carrying offerings . . .

The art of this troubled time was of the people, and has the faults that the phrase implies, but its naive spontaneity has an undeniable charm.

THE MIDDLE KINGDOM (c. 2160-1785 BC)

The classic period of Egypt's greatness

The Middle Kingdom is essentially the history of the 11th and 12th dynasties. Its founder was Mentuhotep I, fourth king of the Theban line; he assumed the double crown and, after the conquest of the delta, ruled over the entire country. His long reign, lasting almost half a century, was extremely active and successful. He transferred the powers of the nomarchs to a vizier resident at court; he reconquered Nubia. His successor Mentuhotep II is almost unkown. Mentuhotep III gradually restored peace to the country. He sent, under the leadership of his vizier Amenemhet, an expedition of ten thousand men across the eastern desert; the object was to exploit the mines of Sinai and to establish trade with the Land of Punt (modern Somalia). Amenemhet created an artificial oasis at Wadi Hamamet, peopled by raids among the Bedouins. He then used the support of the discontented nomarchs to seize power and establish the 12th dynasty.

Amenemhet's first concern was to review the country's political and administrative machinery. To secure his authority he left Thebes and fixed his residence between Memphis and Fayyum. He was obliged, in recompense for the help they had given him, to restore the authority of the provincial governors, but he took care to define their powers exactly. The post of governor ceased to be hereditary and remained in the gift of the king; the boundaries of nomes and provinces were determined by the central government. Some years before his death Amenemhet associated with him his son Sesostris as co-ruler.

He protected Egypt from Asian invaders from east of the delta by building a fortified line of defence known as the "walls of the Ruler." He fought in Sinai and southern Palestine, and reconquered much of Nubia. Resting on the secure basis established by Amenemhet, the 12th dynasty (from about 1991 BC) maintained a rich and powerful state for more than two centuries. This period is one of the greatest in Egypt's history and in the history of civilisation.

Amenemhet was the victim of a palace revolution which caused his son Sesostris to return hurriedly from Libya to claim the throne. In the reign of Sesostris Nubia was colonised as far as the third cataract. Warned by experience of the risks attendant on the succession, Sesostris extended the custom, generally observed by those who followed him, of associating the heir apparent with the throne. Subsequent kings of the dynasty maintained amicable relationships with the rulers of Asia, developed the Fayyum valley, annexed Lower Nubia and systematically worked the mines of Sinai. The peaceful Amenemhet III built, at the entry to Fayyum, a palace of which the size and splendour amazed the first Greek visitors. They called it the Labyrinth.

The last sovereigns of this line lacked calibre, and the decline of the dynasty marked the end of one of the most brilliant periods in the civilisation of the pharaohs.

Changes in the hierarchy of the gods

When, in the course of his struggles with the kings of Heracleopolis, the Theban Intef II seized Abydos, he secured his position by installing the very popular cult of Osiris. It was then that Osiris became definitely identified as the god of the dead.

When Thebes supplanted Heracleopolis, Amenemhet I promoted Amon, god of Thebes, as head of the pantheon. Amon rapidly absorbed the attributes of Re, the divinity of Heliopolitan theology, under the name of Amon-Re, for whom the Theban clergy elaborated a remarkable theology. Amon-Re was creator of all other gods; he was unique, and had neither beginning nor end. He was portrayed as a human being, his head surmounted by two high plumes, often with the sun disk. He was given, as wife, Mut the vulture goddess, and as son, Khons, the moon god. He was the chief of a group of nine gods, modelled on the nine of Heliopolitan theology. His name, which is etymologically related to a word meaning "to hide," suggests the idea of man's incapacity to penetrate the divine nature. He required man, whom he had created, to submit to the universal order of god. He preserved the strength of the mighty and listened to the oppressed; he "watched over sleeping humanity, seeking the good of his flock."

An administration of the highest order

The ability and energy of the 12th dynasty restored Egypt's greatness. Her rulers vigorously promoted the concept of divine authority which had assisted the Old Kingdom. The reigning monarch was identified with the sun; he made fruitful the land and all who served him; total love and obedience were therefore due to him. With equal zeal the dynasty set about the rehabilitation of the state. Although Amenemhet had been obliged to re-establish the position of "High Chief" of the nome, this concession was temporary; the office was suppressed in many areas and virtually eliminated by Sesostris II. The nomarchs, taken as a whole, were good administrators and created a prosperous state.

The kings of the 12th dynasty reorganised government; they also paid much attention to revising the land register and putting into motion the execution of great public works. They methodically and fully exploited the country's resources; one of their most important projects was to reclaim land in the Fayyum depression. This large oasis, on the western border of Middle Egypt, receives its water from a secondary branch of the Nile, the Bahr Yusuf; this empties itself at the foot of the depression into a great lake, the Birkat Qarun, called by the Greeks Lake Moeris. The capital Sheder (the Crocodilopolis of the Greeks), consecrated to the crocodile god Sebek, lay beside the lake. The region was famous for its marshes and woodlands, which furnished the country with quantities of fresh and salt fish, and provided also a hunting ground for the king and his nobles.

Under the 12th dynasty a system of canals converted the Fayyum valley into the most fertile region of Egypt, which it remains to this day. Sesostris II built a dam to protect the valley from flooding at high water, and a sluice to regulate the flow at the point where the Bahr Yusuf entered the oasis. These and other works made the province a model of agricultural efficiency.

An art in scale with man

In the realm of the arts the Middle Kingdom strove to reawaken the spirit of the pyramid builders, the golden age of Egyptian civilisation. If its achievements lack the grandeur of the Old Kingdom they nonetheless possess a truth and delicacy which make this period one of the finest in the history of Egyptian art.

No temples of this period survive, the pharaohs of the 18th dynasty having destroyed them in building larger and finer ones. Very fortunately a large chamber of the time of Sesostris I was discovered in the foundations of the third pylon of the Temple of Amon at Karnak. This little kiosk, built for the Sed festival of the king, has been re-erected at Karnak. It is an elegant pavilion in white limestone, approached by a double staircase and ornamented with reliefs of great delicacy and refinement. This exquisite building is unusual in Egyptian art in its domestic scale.

The royal pyramids, which were built of brick, have not survived. Stone seems to have been reserved for temples. In the provinces important officials built great chapels cut into the rock. These were decorated with animated scenes of daily life: hunting, fishing, farming, games and festivities. One often finds that the architecture of temple entrances is supported by columns of a type called by Champollion "proto-Doric."

Two very different schools are distinguishable in sculpture. The statues from the workshops of Memphis have an elegant and charming stylisation, but they lack vigour and betray a conventional and academic quality; the finest is that of Amenemhet III, found at Hawara. The sculpture of the south shows vigorous realism and a concern to capture likeness; the Theban sculptors delineated the features with superb assurance – as in the fine mask of Sesostris III in the Metropolitan Museum. The statues of private persons, though inferior to those of the kings, show great liveliness of expression and delicacy of modelling.

In the decorative arts jewellery is especially remarkable. Pectorals, rings, amulets, bracelets, diadems, and necklaces are superb; the Egyptian goldsmiths surpassed themselves and achieved perfection.

In this period literature flourished remarkably. The ancient Egyptians always placed a high value upon it, for it bestowed immortality upon its author. A literary legacy, transmitted from generation to generation, formed the basis of the instruction given in the colleges of scribes. Only three genres are known from the Old Kingdom: religious poems (hymns and addresses to the dead); moral teachings, of which, despite their former abundance, we have only those of Ptahotep; and biography, which enabled the kings and nobles to render their account to the gods of the next world. The literature of the Old Kingdom reflected perfect security, an unshakeable faith in the might and duration of its civilisation. But the upheavals that followed shattered this confidence, and produced a doubt and anguish perceptible in later writings. The most frequent literary forms of the Middle Kingdom were Instructions, Prophecies and Tales. The first differ from the traditional instructions in being written by a different type of person. They present advice given by kings to their sons; a mixture of moral and political counsels that exhibit a shrewd knowledge of the human heart. The *Instructions to Merikare*, one of the classics of Egyptian literature, is of great documentary interest, for it describes the political situation in Egypt which preceded the Theban attack on Heracleopolis. The Prophecies narrated past events, usually of a dramatic kind, as if they were still to come, drawing from them a lesson for the future. The sombre events of the First Intermediary Period furnished the authors with material which has proved to be of inestimable value to historians. Two circumstantial works, *The Warnings of an Egyptian Sage* and *The Prophecies of Neferti* describe the social changes that led to the rise of the 12th dynasty. Like the Biblical prophecies the end of the latter work announces the coming of a saviour (Amenemhet I), but with the difference that the coming had already taken place. The Tales show great zest and imagination; the authors found their subjects in history, legend or invention, and told them with a wealth of everyday detail that is lacking in official documents. Among the most celebrated are *The Story of Sinuhe*, which is based on fact; *The Tale of a Peasant*; and the philosophical and pessimistic *Dialogue of a man, tired of life, with his soul.*

Simple, precise and factual, the literature of the Middle Kingdom makes it clear that by this time the art in Egypt was very highly developed. Scientific interests (medical and mathematical) are also found.

THE SECOND INTERMEDIARY PERIOD (1785-1580 BC)

This period, lasting two centuries between the 12th and the 18th dynasties, is the most obscure in Egypt's history. Under the increasingly feeble rulers of the 13th dynasty (1785-1680 BC), and of the still less effective 14th dynasty, the country disintegrated. From the close of the eighteenth century to the beginning of the sixteenth it was dominated by Asiatic invaders. Finally it was liberated by the Princes of Thebes.

In the first phase Egypt seems to have become two kingdoms once again. In the present state of our knowledge it is almost impossible to establish a chronology of the kings. Manetho gives this period the debatable duration of 184 years, perhaps because of the very numerous brief reigns. The king's authority extended over parts of the country only, suggesting the existence of rival dynasties, of which the most powerful was that of Thebes. Whilst weak government left the country defenceless, nomadic tribes began to infiltrate the delta. Their invasions were augmented by the great migrations of peoples taking place in Asia itself. An important document, the stele from Tanis known as "the stele of the year 400," which was erected under Ramses II, enables the first appearance of these invaders and the founding of their capital Avaris to be dated to around 1730 BC. Manetho calls them "shepherds" or "shepherd kings," misinterpreting the name "Hyksos" which in Egyptian means "chiefs of foreign lands." Each year fresh migrations swelled the numbers of Asian invaders in Egypt. Modelling themselves on the Egyptians, they formed a state with a single leader, and set about the conquest of Egypt. This they easily achieved, due to their superior weapons, their horses and war chariots. The 15th and 16th dynasties were made up of Hyksos kings. This crushing defeat left profound traces on the Egyptian spirit, becoming a classic theme of literature.

Little is known of these foreign rulers. After the liberation everything that could recall this dreadful period was destroyed. We know that they were divided into two groups: the "greater" and the "lesser" to whom the whole country rendered tribute.

Certain of the nomarchs of Upper Egypt, themselves to a greater or lesser degree vassals of the Hyksos, became kings by election; their power was circumscribed by the king of Thebes, also a vassal, but they were to a certain degree independent of the Hyksos king. At first their objective was to develop and strengthen their own government; then when the moment came they openly confronted their conquerors. The first to make an attempt, Sekenenre, was killed in the struggle. He was followed by Kamose, who reconquered the country as far as Memphis, capturing the fifteenth, sixteenth and seventeenth nomes. The Hyksos chariots fled in disorder before him.

The final liberation was achieved in the reign of Ahmose. He laid siege to Avaris, the principal Hyksos stronghold, stormed it and sacked it. The Hyksos were driven out of Egypt into southern Palestine. Here Ahmose besieged them in the town of Sharuhen, which he captured after three years.

The partial independence enjoyed by the principality of Thebes enabled it to retain the worship of Amon. Elsewhere the Hyksos tried to impose the cult of their national god Baal, who was identified with Seth.

Administratively the country was divided into provinces which were grouped into two administrative regions – the northern and southern districts. The posts of nomarch were sold and became hereditary.

The decay of central authority meant, as always in Egypt, a decline in the arts. They lost all originality. The rare objects which have survived from the southern region are poor imitations of earlier styles. In the rest of the country, which had been directly in the power of the Hyksos, the total destruction makes it impossible for us to judge the quality of artefacts.

THE NEW KINGDOM (1580-1085 BC)

The power and the glory

The New Kingdom is incontestably the most glorious in the history of the pharaohs, when Egypt extended her empire over wide stretches of Asia. The time had now passed when she could protect herself from invasion by relying on punitive forays and trading alliances, without an efficient, organised military strength. On her eastern frontiers empires were being shaped and reshaped which could rival her strength and threaten her security. A bitter lesson had been learned from the Hyksos occupation; Egypt had now to defend herself by planting garrisons wherever possible and by maintaining her supremacy over subject dynasties. Their weakness was a guarantee of peace.

The wide foreign contacts which this policy entailed affected all aspects of Egyptian culture, religious, artistic, literary, social and military. Furthermore, her vast empire brought fabulous wealth and a taste for luxury greater than had ever been known. The economic benefits of her foreign policy proved to be even greater than did the political advantages.

An urgent task: the reform of home affairs

After defeating the Hyksos, Ahmose, founder of the 18th dynasty, retained Thebes as his capital. His first task was the reorganisation of the debilitated country. By strenuous efforts he succeeded in restoring the economy, helped by the support of a people elated by victory and confident of the future. In gratitude to the gods who had brought him victory, Ahmose restored and rebuilt the temples. By his marriage with his sister Ahmose-Nofretari, a remarkable woman who became a cult figure (women played an important role under this dynasty), he had a son Amenophis I, who succeeded in about 1558 BC. Continuing the work of his father, Amenophis became the architect of the Egyptian empire; he was later associated with the cult of his mother. His two sons predeceased him, causing a disputed succession. Thutmosis I, the son of a concubine, seized power. Having no right to the throne, he legitimised his claim by marrying the hereditary princess. Two daughters were born of this marriage, which posed anew the problem of the succession. Again, the hereditary princess Hatshepsut married her illegitimate brother, who succeeded as Thutmosis II in around 1520 BC. On his death in 1505 he left two daughters and an illegitimate son, then a child, who succeeded as Thutmosis III and married the legitimate daughter of Hatshepsut.

Hatshepsut was an ambitious woman; she declared herself regent and became the effective ruler for twenty-two years – from 1505 till 1483. To guard against the anti-feminist faction, largely composed of certain priests of Amon, she placed her loyal adherents in key government posts; the most renowned were her favourite Semnut, architect of the temple of Deir el Bahari, and Hapuseneb, vizier and high priest of Amon. In an attempt to legitimise her power Hatshepsut proclaimed herself the daughter of Amon, who had personally decreed her rule. She dressed as a man, wore a false beard, and adopted all the royal protocol with the exception of the title "mighty bull." Unfitted by her sex to lead an army she abandoned a policy of conquest in favour of trading expeditions; the most famous was that to the Land of Punt, immortalised in the magnificent reliefs of her temple at Deir el Bahari.

After the death of Hatshepsut in 1483 Thutmosis III was able at last to assume power. Abhorrence of the usurper's memory led him to strike out her name wherever it had been set and substitute his own, or his father's or grandfather's. He died in 1450 BC, after a long reign in which Egypt reached the summit of her power and glory. To avoid any dynastic strife Thutmosis had taken care to associate his son Amenophis II in the throne. The latter was endowed with unusual strength, and an energy tinged with cruelty. He was well able to manage the empire bequeathed to him by his father. The many fine monuments which he has left indicate a prosperous and successful reign. His son Thutmosis IV, who does not seem to have been the natural successor to the throne (he was not the eldest son), is associated with the reclaiming of the Sphinx of Giza from the sand; this achievement is commemorated in a stele, found between its paws, which tells how the prince kept his promise to the sun god to undertake restoration should he become king. His reign was short; he died in 1408 BC and was followed by his son Amenophis III.

Egypt was now the richest and mightiest country of the area, but the indolence of this prince put her position in jeopardy. His queen Teje, who was not of royal blood, had a powerful and often unfortunate influence upon him. He lived in excessive luxury and was energetic only in the hunting of lions. He built a sumptuous palace to the west of Thebes, where he lived surrounded by a court of elaborate protocol and a harem of foreign princesses. The reliefs of the Theban necropolis – some of the very finest – and the colonnades of Luxor testify to the artistic refinement of his reign. The huge funerary temple, of which only the two so-called colossi of Memnon remain, illustrates his taste for the magnificent, which the architect Amenhotep, son of Hapu, satisfied so brilliantly. Shortly before his death it seems he abdicated in favour of his son Amenophis IV, who was then twelve years old. At this time his relations with the priests of Amon began to deteriorate. These had grown very powerful through the benefactions of previous kings and they now presumed to interfere in affairs of state. It was almost certainly for this reason that he removed to a new palace on the opposite banks of the Nile. While honouring the traditional gods he was personally devoted, not to the all-powerful Amon-Re, but to Aton, the sun disk.

The schism of Aton

The new cult of Aton provided the point of departure for the sweeping reform of Amenophis IV. Four years after his succession, in 1366, he decided, after a bitter dispute with the priests of Amon in the course of which he deprived the high priest of control of his secular assets, to abandon Thebes for a new capital, Akhetaton, 360 km downstream at Tell-el-Amarna. The city was dedicated to the sun god Aton, whom the whole country was to worship exclusively. The king took the name of Akhenaton, "He who is pleasing to Aton."

Akhenaton's quarrel with the priests of Amon was only one of the elements conducing to religious change. The previous two centuries of Egyptian expansion had involved the modification of traditional ideas. The mixed races of the empire sought a more universal religion than the specifically Egyptian cult of Amon. All ancient peoples have worshipped the sun in one form or another; Egypt received the cult of Aton, the sun disk, from Asia during the reign of Thutmosis IV. The cult developed, alongside Egypt's many others, under Amenophis III. Akhenaton's radicalism consisted in making it an exclusive monotheism requiring the suppression of Amon and all the lesser gods. The king was the high priest of the new religion; he alone knew and interpreted its doctrines. In all this he was assisted by his wife Nefertiti. Freedom, simplicity, love of nature and joyfulness of spirit were the characteristics of the new faith.

Towards the end of his reign, Akhenaton seems to have attempted a reconciliation with the priests of Amon. The approach, made perhaps under the influence of his mother Queen Teje, caused a breach with Nefertiti. Having no sons, the king chose his son-in-law, Semenkhare, to succeed him. He had a peculiar fondness for Semenkhare, whom he despatched to negotiate with the priests of Amon. The result of his embassy is not known.

Akhenaton and Semenkhare died at a short interval of each other; another son-in-law, Tutankhaton, succeeded. For unknown reasons he left Tell-el-Amarna after three years, and returned to Thebes. There he officially renounced his past errors of faith and took the name of Tutankhamen. He died, after a reign of nine years, at the age of eighteen. The following king, Ay, was a former minister of Akhenaton, who succeeded through his marriage to Tutankhamen's widow. His reign was even briefer; he was replaced by Horemheb, a general of Akhenaton. Horemheb had been sent on a mission to Asia, returning covered in glory. He used his strong position to intrigue with the priests of Amon. These continued to distrust

Akhenaton's successors, who retained a sympathy for the heresy they had renounced, and who refused to persecute the cult of Aton. Having given proof of his orthodoxy, Horemheb was endorsed by an oracle of Amon and elected king. For reasons that were largely political he destroyed all traces of the recent heresy. He then reordered the country's administration which the total indifference of Akhenaton and his successors had plunged into a state of anarchy. The stele known as the stele of Horemheb, found at Karnak, lists the severe penalties decreed by the king for acts of social injustice.

The glorious reign of the Ramessides

It is not known if Horemheb was related to his successor Ramses I, who founded the 19th dynasty. Ramses was a member of a noble family of the delta area, which came, perhaps, from the reign of Tanis. This is suggested by the prominence given to the cult of Seth at this time. Though hated by the Egyptians since the time of the Hyksos, the god had continued to be worshipped in this region; his cult was taken up by the new sovereigns who made Tanis their summer residence. The father of Ramses I was called Seti, meaning man of Seth; he had been "chief of the archers" in the army. His son followed him in the post, and was covered with honours by Horemheb, who no doubt nominated him as his heir. Ramses's son – the future Seti I – was vizier of Horemheb, and among other priestly functions was high priest of Seth.

Ramses I reigned for only sixteen months, about which we know very little. Under his successors, Seti I (1312-1298 BC), Ramses II (1298-1235 BC) and Merneptah (1235-1224 BC), home affairs seem to have been uneventful. The kings were warriors and diplomats, though this did not prevent their being also great builders with a taste for the colossal.

Towards the end of the reign of Merneptah, decadence brought a decline in prosperity. The following kings were largely usurpers. For a quarter of a century Egypt went through an internal crisis in which anarchy prevailed. Order was restored through the initiative of Sethnakht, a man of unknown origin who founded the 20th dynasty. His son, Ramses III, was the last great ruler of Egypt. He totally reorganised the administration of the country, restructuring government appointments and dividing the population into a number of classes: palace officials, nobles, soldiers and artisans. Prosperity returned with the regular flow of taxes; trade and diplomacy were resumed and new temples built (Medinet Habu).

Ramses III was the victim, late in life, of a conspiracy among his entourage, and appears to have been assassinated. Of his son, Ramses IV, and the seven other kings of that name who followed we know little, except that their reigns witnessed a decadence which was aggravated by quarrels over the succession. Famine, the violation of royal tombs, and serious trouble in Middle Egypt from Libyan invasions all occurred. The kings shared their royal prerogatives with the priests of Amon who eventually came to dominate the ancient monarchy of Thebes.

The conquest of an empire

The New Kingdom pursued a policy of conquest. After throwing out the Hyksos, Ahmose waged three wars to subdue Nubia and imposed an Egyptian protectorate on the Phoenician ports. Amenophis I and Thutmosis I extended the empire into the Sudan; Thutmosis II probably reached Napata near the fourth cataract. These distant campaigns, of which the kings of Egypt liked to boast, probably amounted to no more than a few punitive expeditions.

Asian affairs were the most pressing concern of the New Kingdom rulers. For five centuries they contended with three major enemies in this region: the Mitannians, the Hittites and the Sea Peoples. Amenophis I was the true architect of the Egyptian Empire; on his death it extended from Upper Nubia to the Euphrates. Thutmosis I and II maintained this supremacy, promptly suppressing sporadic revolts. Egypt, however, kept no occupying force in the Asian provinces; she exacted an annual tribute and maintained a few garrisons. The twenty-five years of dynastic strife that followed the death of Thutmosis II allowed the Mitannians – Aryan conquerors of the region east of the Euphrates – to gain ascendancy. They formed an anti-Egyptian federation of the 330 odd kings, princelings and chieftains who ruled Palestine and Syria. It cost the energetic Thutmosis III seventeen campaigns to put an end to this Asian coalition. This he achieved by an acute political strategy; he returned each year to Asia, to suppress or prevent revolts, and formed fruitful alliances with the defeated chiefs. The final coalition, formed in 1464 BC by the Mitannian king and the Hittite prince of Kadesh, one of Egypt's fieriest opponents, was broken by the siege and capture of Kadesh. Egyptian power was now at its zenith. In the fifty-four glorious years of his reign Thutmosis III finally established Egypt's mastery over western Asia; the Assyrian, Hittite and Babylonian peoples sent tribute, and Egypt's troops and booty passed through Phoenician ports.

Thutmosis III's successor Amenophis II suppressed two revolts in Asia, bringing home immense booty and many prisoners, including seven Syrian princes. Six were sacrificed to Amon at Thebes and the seventh at Napata. This savagery, Asian in tradition, had an effect on the subject peoples; peace ensued for a time. Thutmosis IV made an alliance with the Mitannians intended to thwart the growing power of the Hittites; he married the daughter of the Mitannian king. The Nile valley was now at its most prosperous; incalculable wealth flowed into its coffers, allowing the construction of sumptuous monuments and the creation of works of art which speak of the elegance and refinement of Egypt at the height of her civilisation.

Unhappily for the country the next pharaoh, Amenophis III, had no taste for war; he relied on the fidelity of the vassal states. While he enjoyed the luxury of an oriental despot the vassal princes begged for help against Hittite and Aramaean attacks. The collapse of Mitannian power, which occurred shortly after the death of Akhenaton, enabled the Hittites to attack the Egyptians in Syria and Palestine. Tutankhamen dispatched General Horemheb to restore the situation; he reclaimed Palestine but went no further, wisely deciding to consolidate Egypt's position there.

An aggressive foreign policy was resumed under the 19th dynasty. Seti I suppressed a rebellion of Bedouins, who had seized forts along the military route from El Kantara to Gaza. He went on to Canaan to combat a dangerous coalition formed by the Hittites. By brilliant tactics he disposed of his enemies before they could join forces, thus making himself master of a large part of Palestine. In further campaigns he defeated the Hittites at Kadesh and repulsed an attack.

His successor Ramses II also contended chiefly with the Hittites. By intimidation or bribery they had engineered the most formidable coalition Egypt had yet faced. Ramses was caught in a critical situation at Kadesh, when part of his force was captured from the rear. The occasion was saved by the courage and leadership of the king. This famous action was commemorated in the epic poem, the "Poem of Pentaur," and illustrated in the great temples of Karnak and Luxor, in the Ramesseum and at Abydos. In 1278 BC the Egyptians and Hittites were drawn together by the common fear of the growing power of Abyssinia. They signed a treaty at Tanis in the twenty-first year of the reign of Ramses II. Peace ensued for twenty-five years, no country daring to challenge the combined strength of Egypt and the Hittite empire. The marriage of Ramses II to a Hittite princess in 1264 BC was the occasion of great celebrations.

Towards the end of this reign a great movement of peoples took place in the Balkans and the Black Sea region. The Indo-European Sea Peoples swept down through Greece and the Aegean into Asia Minor and Libya. The Hittite empire collapsed before them. The tribes that had entered Libya found that country too poor, and moved into the Nile valley, penetrating almost to Memphis. In a battle lasting six hours they were routed by Merneptah leaving 9,000 prisoners and much booty. Merneptah's subsequent reconquest of perpetually insurgent Palestine is recorded in the celebrated "stele of Israel."

Under Ramses III the army was reorganised to meet the constant threat of the Sea Peoples. The king checked a fresh invasion from Libya in 1193 BC, and brilliantly defeated a further threat from the east by a combined sea and land attack. The invaders were dispersed, with the exception of the Philistines who settled the coastal strip between Gaza and Mount Karmel. Ramses III maintained control to the east and west, but under his successors Egypt's authority in Asia became progressively feebler.

The tools of power: monarchy, army, government

The concept of monarchy by divine right, through descent from the god, was supplemented in the New Kingdom by recourse to theogamy: the union of the god with a human bride, her power being legitimised by divine election. The god's decision was confirmed by the priests of Amon, the acknowledged interpreters of his will. The priests were quick to profit from their new role, which gave them unique power. Enriched by bequests from the conquering pharaohs, they became a state within the state.

Though still an absolute monarch, pharaoh could not personally deal with all his functions. These he delegated to senior ministers. When the king was strong and skilful in the selection and control of his deputies, this dispersal of power was not detrimental; it became dangerous in the hands of a weakling.

The pharaohs of the New Kingdom had an additional responsability, that of head of the army. During the time of the Old and Middle Kingdom the country had no standing army; the nomarchs would raise a force whenever necessary. Only the police, largely recruited in Nubia, formed a permanent force. With the expansionist policy of the New Kingdom a professional army became essential. It was composed of two large battalions, garrisoned in the delta area and in Upper Egypt. In time of war it was divided into four regiments, supplemented by mercenaries. Each regiment was under the protection of a major god: the army of Amon, the army of Re, the army of Ptah – to which Ramses II added the army of Seth. The infantry was supported by the chariot corps, which employed two-manned vehicles drawn by two horses. The army was co-ordinated by a supreme commander usually of royal birth; the fresh and salt-walter fleets were commanded by an admiral. Members of the army received grants of land for their peacetime maintenance, on which they rapidly grew rich.

Expansion into Asia and Africa caused an increase in government administration. Two viziers were appointed, a southern vizier at Thebes and a northern at Heliopolis. The viziers were responsible for the judiciary, the treasury, the record office and all public services, as well as for supplying the armed forces. In general they were conscientious and contributed much to the country.

As a result of the reconquest of the southern empire, the post of viceroy of Nubia was created. The country was divided into two huge provinces, Nubia proper and Kush (modern Sudan). Its government was modelled on that of Egypt, and was presided over by the viceroy. Nubia supplied Egypt with gold from Kush, ivory, ebony, giraffes, monkeys, ostriches, ostrich plumes and leopard skins. From the time of the 18th dynasty Nubia became Egyptianised. Nubian princes were often educated at the pharaoh's court, and took home the culture of the metropolis; many Nubians worked in central government. The post of viceroy was an exalted one, carrying the title of "Overseer of the Southern Land" or "Royal Son of Kush." Its holders were in the main extremely able men.

In the Asian provinces no attempt was made to impose Egyptian forms of government. Local traditions were respected, Egypt intervening only as arbiter between the principalities. Her military presence was limited to a few outposts. Asian crown princes were often brought up at the Egyptian court, an effective way of disseminating Egyptian influence. The Asian provinces bore a heavy burden of taxation: grain, oil, wine, livestock, gold, silver, copper, precious woods, horses, slaves. In war the Egyptian army was billeted upon them. The wealth and refinement of Egypt's civilisation was based largely on tribute from the east. An unlooked for consequence of the extension eastwards was the perfecting of the art of embalming through the use of Asian aromatic substances. The best preserved mummies are those of the New Kingdom.

An art worthy of Egypt's grandeur

The fabulous wealth of Egypt resulted in a great architectural flowering. Its traces can be seen in the innumerable temples that line the Nile from the third cataract all the way to the delta. Their plan usually consists of a colonnaded court, a hypostyle hall, and one or more sanctuaries. At the entrance is a pylon (a monumental gateway flanked by towers) preceded by two obelisks, symbols of the sun. The temples of the 18th dynasty were directly inspired by those of the Middle Kingdom. Their sober elegance is often enhanced by the grandeur of their setting, such as that of the temple of Hatshepsut at Deir el Bahari. In the time of Akhenaton's religious reform the usual progression within the temple from daylight to dark was abandoned in favour of a building open to the light. A system of open courtyards and corridors led to the sanctuary where the altar stood, bathed in sunlight.

The 19th dynasty favoured the colossal in architecture, but not at the expense of harmony; the magnificent Hypostyle Hall at Karnak is a fine example. In Nubia rock-cut temples predominate, the most famous being that built by Ramses II at Abu Simbel.

For their tombs the kings of the 18th dynasty created subterranean chambers in the rock of the western desert. The burial chamber was usually at a considerable depth; it was approached by a gently sloping corridor which widened on occasions to form two small symmetrical chambers. The Valley of the Tombs of the Kings has a counterpart in the Valley of the Queens. The tombs of subjects consisted of a chapel, usually cut in the rock, which was preceded by a court or a vertical shaft leading to the tomb. A brick pyramid, the royal sun symbol, now appropriated by subjects, stood at the entrance to the chapels.

The figures seen in mural decorations now become elongated, giving the works of this period their incomparable elegance and distinction. The form is exquisitely controlled; idealisation does not preclude a degree of realism. These works have never been surpassed.

Akhenaton's Amarnian revolution, which rejected all tradition, adopted an often brutal realism; the spirituality and love of nature which also characterised the movement is reflected in works of an affecting charm and sensitivity. The intense inner life, the vividness of detail freely and naturalistically rendered, the felicitous freedom seen in the works of the Amarnian artists are unique in Egyptian art. Unhappily, they vanish with the suppression of the heresy.

The traditional manner returned with Seti I; it produced reliefs of a sensitivity and purity of outline that place them amongst the great Egyptian achievements. Gradually, however, the style ossified into mere imitation.

The royal statues of the New Kingdom have an elegance given by the elongation of the bodies and dignity of stance, but there is a certain lack of definition in the features. The Amarnian statues, on the other hand, portray the features of Akhenaton with a realism infused with inner intensity, a spirituality which has a tinge of melancholy. The sensitivity and charm of the two superb portraits of Nefertiti, at Cairo and Berlin, rightly place them amongst the world's masterpieces.

A less extreme Amarnian style lingered for a short time; it is seen in fine works like the statue of Tutankhamen and the head of General Horemheb. Though some good work in the traditional manner was produced during the 19th dynasty, the style later became decadent.

Two minor arts deserve mention. The first was that of funeral papyri, which guided the dead in after-life; these were illustrated by remarkable vignettes, often in colour. The second was that of the ostraka, which were used something in the manner of sketchbooks: their humour and invention gives them unusual charm.

The minor arts reflected the nation's wealth. The over-elaborate jewellery falls short of that of the Middle Kingdom. Ornate beds and chairs of refined design were produced. Elaborate formal dress, elegant sandals, heavy curled wigs and long pleated tunics for women appeared. Toilet objects were exquisitely designed and made.

In literature an important development occurred: the classical written language lost ground to that of everyday speech. When the scribes began to write in the vulgar tongue the usage spread rapidly, and the literary form became a dead language. Among the many literary genres one of the most popular was the epic which celebrated kingly deeds, such as the poem of Pentaur. These were still written in the classical tongue and they provide much information about foreign campaigns. Another popular form was the hymn, addressed to a god or a king. Akhenaton's "Hymns to the Sun" stand apart from the rest. Their mysticism. their joyous praise of nature, and their poetic stature allies them with certain Psalms of David.

Tales of all kinds continued to be very popular. The refinement and delicacy of the New Kingdom can be perceived in the "Songs of Love," dialogues between lover and loved one which are very close to the Song of Songs.

THE LATE DYNASTIC PERIOD (1085-333 BC)

The Decline

This period, a period of decadence, extended from the 21st dynasty to the conquest of Alexander. Feeble sovereigns were forced to share royal power with a growing number of almost independent dynasties. Egypt's severe internal anarchy caused her to lose all prestige and to fall under foreign domination. Though Thebes remained the religious capital, the centre of activity moved north. An active foreign policy and the ancient suzerainty over Asia were abandoned. The process of decline evolved in several stages.

The theocratic dictatorship of the priest-kings

The 21st dynasty (1085-950 BC) was founded by Smendes, a man of unknown origin, who made his capital at the ancient city of Avaris, then known as Tanis.

At Thebes a virtually independent dynasty held power. Its kings were descendants of Herihor, general and trusted minister of Ramses XI, who had appropriated many royal prerogatives as the king allowed them to fall under his control, including that of "chief Prophet of Amon." He had finally managed to secure the right to a royal title. The Tanite sovereigns, including the celebrated Psusennes I, tried to curb Theban power by marrying their daughters to Theban princes, but to no avail. Three of these priest-kings enclosed their names in the pharaonic cartouche. The Theban military pontiffs presided over a theocratic dictatorship; they decided all matters concerning both the living and the dead, through the authority of the oracle of Amon.

The Libyan "feudal" anarchy

The Libyan prince Sheshouk (the Shishak of the Bible) came to the throne in 950 BC, and founded the 22nd Bubastite dynasty. Under the later Ramesside kings the Libyans had peacefully infiltrated the delta area, where they had been recruited as mercenaries; in the time of the priest-kings they became the leading military caste. Their leaders extended their power from Bubastis to Thebes, and had no difficulty in dislodging the preceding dynasty. Sheshouk married his son to the daughter of Psusennes II. He was an able and energetic ruler. Disturbances in Judaea enabled him to enter Palestine; he seized Jerusalem, sacked the Temple and carried off its treasures. His successors were unable to impose their authority on their vassals, who formed a number of virtually independent states. Under the 23rd dynasty, founded by a prince of Bubastis, disruption grew worse until anarchy invited invasion.

The ascendancy of the south

Tefnakte, prince of Sais, founded the 24th dynasty (730-715 BC); he vainly attempted to prevent an invasion from Kush. King Piankhi of Kush appropriated Upper Egypt, and by 715 BC his brother and successor, Shabaka, had gained control of the entire country. He reformed the administration, restored the temples and adopted a policy of conciliation towards the growing power of Abyssinia. The 25th Kushite dynasty (715-659 BC) gave the country half a century of prosperity; its most brilliant ruler was Taharga. Continuous trouble from the northern princes enabled the Assyrians, under Ashurbanipal, to occupy the delta in 663 BC and to sack the city of Thebes.

The Sait renaissance

Egypt was delivered from the Assyrians and Kushites by the king of Sais, Psamtik I, founder of the 26th dynasty (664-525 BC). He suppressed the power of the local princes and reorganised the economy; agriculture throve again and the country experienced its last period of brilliance. The reawakened national spirit revived Egypt's intellectual and artistic traditions; artists drew their inspiration from works of the Old and Middle Kingdoms. The arts achieved a perfection which, though somewhat cold and academic, was yet highly expressive; especially so was the vigorous portraiture, later imitated by the Romans.

Such references to the past did not prevent innovation. Under the pharaohs Necho III, Psamtik II, Apries and Amasis, there were fruitful contacts between Egypt and Greece. Greece profited from Egyptian science and thought; Psamtik II relied on Greek mercenaries as officers in the army. He also procured a fleet of Greek triremes and attracted foreign traders; for the latter he created a corps of interpreters. In 565 BC Naukratis, a Greek free port, was established in the delta.

The Persian oppression

In 525 BC Cambyses, King of Persia, invaded Egypt and annexed the country to the Achaemenian empire. Proclaiming himself pharaoh, he founded the 27th dynasty. He completed the canal between the Nile and the Red Sea, begun under the previous dynasty, and codified Egyptian civil law. There were continuous attempts at revolt; the country was liberated for a short period during which the last three independent dynasties reigned, the 28th (404-395 BC), the 29th (398-378 BC), and the 30th (378-341 BC). This fragile independence was destroyed by rivalries; in 341 BC the Persians overran the country once more. The Persian kings, making no further attempt to accommodate the Egyptian tradition, imposed an iron rule.

THE MACEDONIAN ERA (333-30 BC): HELLENISATION

Alexander the Great and his successors

In the autumn of 333 BC, after his defeat of Darius at Issus, Alexander the Great entered Egypt; he was greeted as a liberator. In a few months he had reorganised the country; he retained existing institutions within a strong framework of Greek fiscal and military organisation. For his new capital, Alexandria, he chose an advantageous coastal site; the city provided the eastern Mediterranean with a new great port. He visited the oasis of Siwa in the western desert to consult the famous oracle of Amon; the god acknowledged him as his son and predicted his world-wide dominion. Alexander then left for the Orient. There he died, in 323 BC, without returning to Egypt (in which he had spent only six months). His body was returned to the capital that he had founded. Neither his brother, Philip, nor his son visited Egypt. Power was delegated to Ptolemy, son of Lagus, who, five years after the death of Alexander II, proclaimed himself king.

The Ptolemaic exploitation

The descendants of Lagus governed Egypt for three centuries; they in some ways call to mind the house of Atreus. Crime became a means of succession and government, the queens enjoying more power and respect than the kings. The Ptolemies preserved the traditional costumes and ceremonies of the pharaohs, and assumed sun-king titles. But under the early sovereigns

Alexandrian culture was exclusively Greek. It showed its brilliance in the founding of the University, the Museum and the Library and the building of the lighthouse of Pharos. The canal to the Red Sea was opened and Greek sailors explored new trade routes. The government was strongly centralised, everything being in the hands of the king, who was assisted by a hierarchy of officials. A bureaucracy of paralysing complexity was highly effective in its objective of extracting enough wealth from the country to maintain an army and fleet which preserved Macedonian supremacy in the Mediterranean. The thirty or so provinces were administered by Egyptian nomarchs, coupled with Greek policy-makers. All important posts were reserved for Greeks. Egyptians were forbidden to settle in cities open to the colonists. Later, when rebellion threatened, the Ptolemaic rulers adopted a more lenient policy; but it was already too late.

The new sovereigns adopted the old Egyptian religion unchanged. Ptolemy I instituted the state worship of the Sacred Bull of Apis, identified with Osiris (known to the Greeks as Serapis), and of his wife Isis and son Horus; the Triad was enthroned with great pomp in the Serapeum at Alexandria. To gain Egyptian sympathy the Ptolemies built their grandiose temples such as those at Edfu and Dendera; they are worthy of the ancient tradition, although they exhibit a certain decadence in their decoration. Throughout the country a hybrid art was produced; it combined Egyptian themes with elements from the Hellenistic culture promoted at Alexandria.

The last and most famous of the Ptolemaic sovereigns was Cleopatra IV, wife of Julius Caesar and later of Mark Antony. After ruinous defeat at Actium in 30 BC and besieged by the Romans under Octavian, she killed herself at Alexandria.

ROMAN AND BYZANTINE DOMINATION (30 BC-640 AD)

On the death of Cleopatra Egypt fell to Augustus, and was for six centuries part of the Roman empire. At first the Romans maintained a military rule; disturbances were severely suppressed, especially the bloodthirsty quarrels between Alexandrians and Jews. Hadrian came to Egypt to repair the ravages and revive Ptolemaic culture; he founded the city of Antinoöpolis on the right bank of the Nile, which had become a centre of Graeco-Roman culture. His successors followed a policy of moderation, but unrest and repression recurred; under the Severi persecution of the Christians developed. Egypt, whose grain surpluses had made her the granary of Rome, now experienced a period of social and economic instability.

Augustus and his successors continued the tradition of building temples to the local gods, on which they had themselves depicted in the Egyptian manner. They must be given credit for an architectural jewel, the temple of Isis on the island of Philae. Begun under the Ptolemies, it was miraculously saved from the waters of the old Aswan dam when the new dam was completed in 1970. A new development of this period was that of the portraits on wood, originating in the Fayyum region; they were applied to the coffins of mummies.

The Alexandrian cult of Serapis was brought to Rome and spread throughout the empire. In Egypt itself it was submerged by the rising tide of Christianity, and disappeared rapidly after the Edict of Theodosius (392 AD) forbade pagan rites.

The accession of Diocletian in 284 marked the beginning of the Byzantine era in Egypt. It saw also the break-up of the country's administrative unity. Its political division was the work of Justinian, promulgated in his ordinance of 538-539. Civil service corruption, religious faction and the growing pressure of taxation so exhausted the Egyptians, and their hatred of both Roman greed and Byzantine severity was such, that they offered but little resistance to the conquering armies of Islam.

50

49. Sunset on the Nile at Luxor.

51

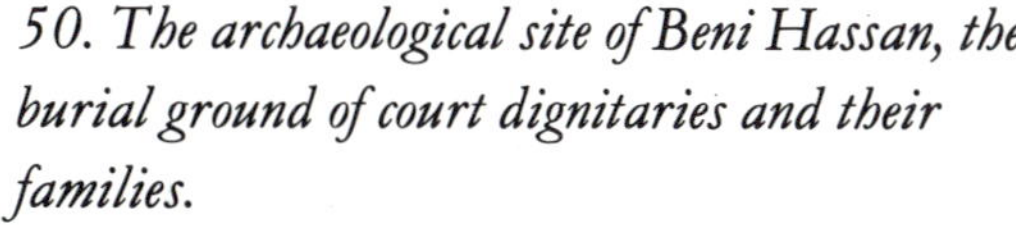

52

53

50. The archaeological site of Beni Hassan, the burial ground of court dignitaries and their families.

51. Bas-relief from the Temple of Horus at Edfu, built in the Ptolemaic period. The Ptolemies, to ingratiate themselves with the people, built several grand temples worthy of the ancient tradition.

52. House in Aswan painted a lively shade of blue. The colour is mixed in with the plaster instead of being applied afterwards.

53. Boat on the shore of Lake Qarun, with the eye of Horus painted on it to ward off evil spirits.

54

5

56

54. A Bedouin and his donkey near the tombs at Sakkara.

55. The interior of the Abu al-Haggag mosque, built on the site of the Temple of Luxor.

56. The wall around the site at Sakkara, where King Djoser's Step Pyramid is, is 600 yards long on the longer sides and over 300 on the shorter ones.

57

58

57. *A pharaonic necropolis at Luxor.*

58. *The Valley of the Kings, on the west bank at Thebes, is a narrow gorge surrounded by sheer rockface. The rulers of the New Kingdom had themselves buried here, in great secret, in underground crypts, some of them 100 yards deep.*

59. *The Step Pyramid at Sakkara. Djoser, a 3rd dynasty king, built the first pyramid in the world: the oldest architecture in stone of which we have knowledge.*

60. *The columns of the Hypostyle Hall in the Temple of Amon-Re at Karnak.*

62

63

61. The First Pylon (or monumental doorway) of the Temple of Amon-Re at Karnak, with one of the many sphinxes that line the entrance passage. Originally there was an avenue of sphinxes from Luxor to Karnak.

62. Valley of the Kings, tomb of Sethnakht, first king of the 20th dynasty.

63. Near the archaeological site at Luxor the buildings are decorated with contemporary murals on a variety of subjects, including figures taken from the ancient temples.

64. The Ramesseum, built by Ramses II, in Luxor.

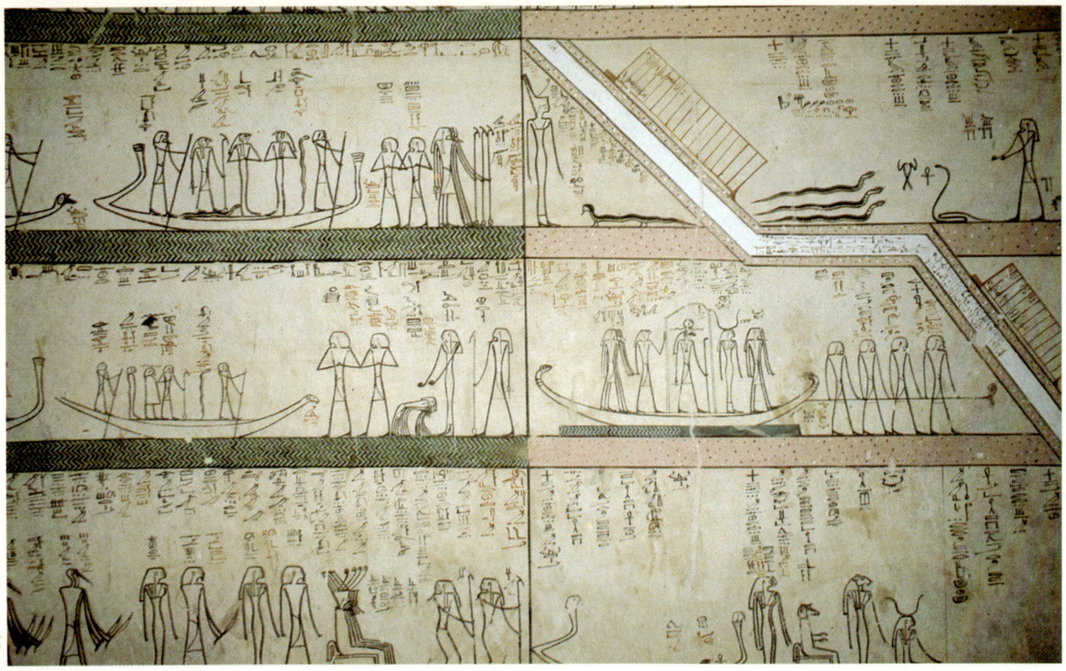

65

66

67

68

65. Painting illustrating the journey of the soul in the tomb of Thutmosis III, in the Valley of the Kings.

66. Writing on the walls in the tomb of Thutmosis III. The essential function of hieroglyphics was to ensure immortality for the things represented, be they names or lists of provisions needed in the after-life. But, apart from these magical properties, the signs were conceived as images to delight the eye: their ordering made a true work of art.

67. Stele from Tell-el-Amarna showing the solar disk and the family of Akhenaton. Cairo Museum.

68. The Pyramid of Cheops, the largest of the Giza pyramids, photographed early in a winter morning. Cheops, the son of Snefru, was the second king of the 4th dynasty and reigned from about 2589 BC for twenty-three years, most of which were probably spent building this pyramid.

69. The paintings on the ceiling of the tomb of Seti I (19th dynasty) represent astrological subjects.

70

71

70. The Pyramid of Khephren. At the top one can still see the remains of the stone facing which once covered all the pyramids.

71. Camels waiting for tourists at Giza.

72 

73 

 74

72. Hatshepsut's mortuary temple, at Deir el Bahari on the west bank at Thebes. Hatshepsut was the daughter of Thutmosis I and for many years was co-regent with her nephew Thutmosis III. During her reign she had this temple built, but when she died Thutmosis III had all her effigies scratched out of the bas-reliefs.

73. A fisherman's boat called Hatshepsut.

74. Painting in the tomb of Seti I.

75. The Temple of Seti I at Abydos. Abydos, in Upper Egypt, was one of the country's most sacred places, where the souls of the dead came from all over Egypt to gather at the tomb of Osiris. The paintings in the mortuary chapels show the souls sailing up the Nile on their mystic voyage.

76

77

76. The minaret of the Abu al-Haggag mosque and the columns of the Temple of Luxor.

77. The Temple of Haroeris and Sebek at Kom Ombo. Being dedicated to two gods, this temple has two entrances and each chamber was divided into two sections. The relief in the foreground shows the king making an offering to Sebek.

78. A guide standing in front of a column at Dendera gives an idea of the scale of these buildings.

79

80

81

82

83

79. The sacred lake of the temple at Dendera. The lakes were connected with the worship of the resurrection of Osiris and all temples had them. This one is the best preserved.

80. Scarab. Vatican, Egyptian Museum.

81. The façade of the Great Temple of Ramses II at Abu Simbel. The four seated figures, more than 20 metres high, are all portrayals of Ramses II. The much smaller figures, between the feet and at the foot of the thrones, are members of his family: his mother, wife and children.

82. The façade of the Small Temple of Abu Simbel, erected in honour of Nefertari, Ramses II's second wife.

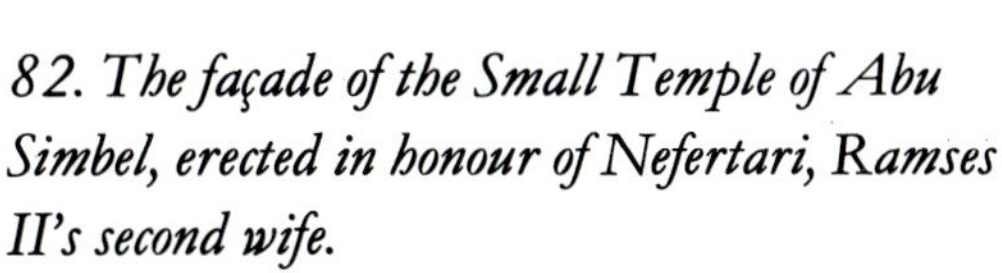

83. Detail of one of the figures from the façade of the Small Temple of Abu Simbel.

Abu Simbel, south of the Aswan dam, is the southernmost point reached by the civilisation of the pharaohs. Its temples, as famous as those at Giza or Karnak, were saved by a committee set up in 1960 by UNESCO. The lake that was created by the Aswan dam flooded the area where these temples stood – but their remarkable façades had been moved to safety.

84. Trajan's pavilion, dedicated to the goddess Isis, on Philae, the sacred island on Lake Nasser.

85

86

87

85. Funerary boat from the tomb of Tutankhamen. Cairo Museum.

86. The Book of the Dead. Turin, Egyptian Museum.

87. A slave grinding corn. Florence, Archaeological Museum.

88. Shauabti, or small figurine, from the tomb of Tutankhamen. Cairo Museum.

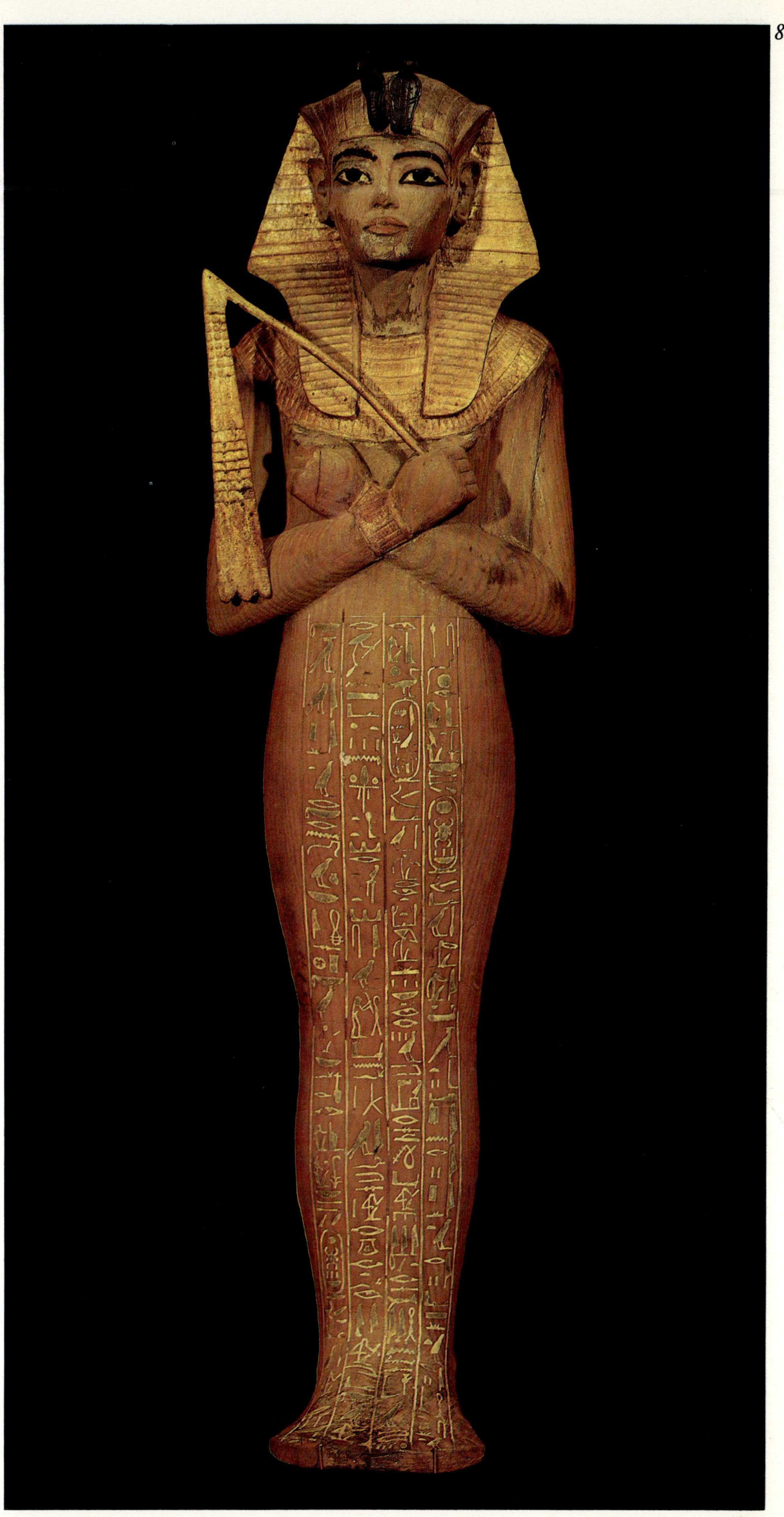

88

89. Portrait of a girl. Florence, Archaeological Museum. Several similar portraits, painted on wood, were found in the Fayyum region; they are the most important artistic production dating from the period of Roman domination.

90. The Pyramids of Giza are visited every year by hordes of tourists and many concessions have been made to this form of mass culture.

Christian Egypt

The word Copt, used today to denote a member of the native Christian church of Egypt, is derived from the Greek name for the country *Aegyptos*, corrupted by the Arabs to Gyptos/Coptos/Copts.

The church of Saint Mark

According to tradition the Egyptian church was founded by Saint Mark. The earliest known reference to this was made in the fourth century by Eusebius in his *Ecclesiastical History*: "They say that Mark was the first apostle to be sent to Egypt, that he preached there the gospel that he had written, and established churches at Alexandria itself." Egypt proved fertile ground for Christianity; the Egyptians, with their longing for inner purity, their religious zeal, and their preoccupation with the future life, were ideally suited to receive such a religion.

Saint Mark made his first converts in the Jewish community of Alexandria. The new religion spread among the Greek, Roman and Egyptian intelligentsia. These were a Hellenised and tolerant people, used to religious syntheses. They had already accepted the amalgamation of Egypt's ancient gods with those of Greece, Rome and the East. All religious speculation converged on one point: the attempts to define the nature of man's relationship with his god.

Christianity might have been in danger of becoming merely one more religion amongst many others. That it did not is due to the fact that, at a very early stage, preaching in the Coptic language was adopted, rather than in Greek. Greek was the language of the elite; Coptic, as we have seen, the language of pharaonic Egypt, written in Greek characters. Through its use, Christianity was able to spread throughout the country and to reach all levels of society. The gnostic texts found in 1946 at Nag Hammadi in Upper Egypt (writings of a sect that believed that creation was an accident for which God compensated by sending his son to save mankind through *gnosis*, or knowledge) show what an important part preaching in Coptic had played in the early centuries.

The crucial role of Alexandria

The first Christian university was founded in Alexandria. That elite and cosmopolitan city, the centre of intellectual activity, was chosen by the patriarchs as the site for an institution intended to set the Christian message against the pagan philosophy enshrined in the Alexandrian Museum and Library. The School of Alexandria, this great theological college, endowed with a library in which the sciences were taught, was meant to show the world that Christian philosophy could rival the achievements of pagan Hellenism. By the end of the second century its reputation was established. It was illuminated by a galaxy of illustrious names: Clement, Origen, Athanasius, Cyril. Their great achievement was to present Christianity not as a rupture with the past, but as its fulfilment, the culmination of all previous mystical movements and philosophies, which in their various ways had prefigured the truth.

The patriarchal seat of Alexandria had a profound influence on the early development of the Christian church. It helped to clarify belief and to formulate dogma. Through its fierce battles against heresy it defined the orthodox. The Ecumenical Council of Nicaea in 325 established the patriarchate of Alexandria as second only to that of Rome; its jurisdiction extended over Egypt, Libya and the Pentapolis. The encyclical which, each year, fixed the date of Easter, was the privilege of the Alexandrian episcopate until the Council of Nicaea, in withdrawing it, struck the first blow against Alexandrian prestige.

The age of the martyrs

The Egyptian church was particularly affected by the Roman persecutions, especially in the third century. Instigated by the hated pagan sovereigns, these served only to strengthen the faith. Cruel though they were, they were interspersed with periods of relative calm; these gave Christianity time to take root and spread.

The persecutions began with Septimus Severus's edict of 202 dissolving the School of

Alexandria, the most active centre of Christian propaganda; it claimed many victims in that city. A much more violent persecution followed in 250, after an edict of Decius had required Christians to proclaim publicly their faith in the pagan cult. The edict was enforced with extreme rigour throughout Egypt, by special commissions. Though some Christians apostasised, many became martyrs. A further edict was issued by Valerian in 258. But, rather than checking the spread of Christianity, these persecutions encouraged it. The most brutal were those instigated, after a respite of forty years, during the reign of Diocletian. These began in 303, intensified under the influence of Galerius in 304, and became yet more horrific after Diocletian's abdication in 305. Eusebius, who witnessed them, speaks of atrocious tortures and mass executions; he cites a figure of ten thousand victims in Upper Egypt, the area most affected.

To commemorate these martyrs the Egyptian Christians dated their era, which they called the Age of the Martyrs, from the year 284, the date of Diocletian's succession.

A temporary end to persecution came with the victory of Constantine over Maxentius in 312 which, according to Christian tradition, finally established Christianity as the official religion of the empire. The Edict of Milan of 313 established freedom of worship. By the middle of the fourth century the Alexandrian Christian community had become extremely important and Christianity was well established throughout the country. In 339 Athanasius estimated the number of Egyptian bishops as approaching a hundred.

Pagan resistance

The old Egyptian religion, meanwhile, continued to have adherents, especially among the intelligentsia. Documentary evidence shows that it was very much alive up to the sixth century, and was still in existence at the time of the Arab conquest. At the beginning of the sixth century paganism attempted a final resistance to the advance of Christianity. This movement, which developed in the precints of the University of Alexandria, had its roots in Egyptian nationalism, in a nostalgia for pharaonic Egypt, and in adherence to tradition and the ancestral religion. To the adherents of intellectual paganism, with its taste for rational speculation, to be pagan was to be truly Egyptian.

During the Greek and Roman occupations Egyptian paganism had lost its cohesive centre. The Ptolemaic court, which contained a number of native Egyptians, had continued to act as a directing and modifying influence on religion. But with the coming of Roman bureaucracy this sense of direction was lost. Temple worship was then addressed not to Pharaoh, son of the mighty sun god, but to the detested Roman emperors who did not even trouble to choose a sun-title. The priests, strongly Hellenised and ignorant of ancient dogma, had no hold over the people. Left to itself, popular belief foundered in magic and superstition. The Edict of Theodosius of 392, in forbidding all pagan rites, destroyed the bond and preserver of belief: religious worship.

Deprived of its temples and its clergy, and exhausted by its struggles with Christianity, paganism gradually lost ground; it sought refuge in isolated corners of Upper Egypt, in the sanctuaries of Isis, and in the University of Alexandria.

Monasticism: an invention of Egypt

During the fourth century a phenomenon of great religious significance occurred in Egypt, when thousands of Christians retreated into the deserts to lead lives of solitude, abstinence and prayer.

This spontaneous movement cannot be explained solely by a desire to escape either persecution or the crushing burden of Byzantine taxation. It is no accident that monasticism was born on the banks of the Nile: ancient Egypt had already known a form of anchoritism. The Theban hills are full of graffiti left by people who, from the time of the 19th dynasty, had sought solitude, visions of Amon and prayer in the silence of the desert. A Greek papyrus of the second century BC, found in the ruins of the necropolis of Memphis, reveals that within the precinct of the famous temple of Serapis lived recluses, kept within the walls by the "divine power," and dedicated to certain rites. Although their nature has not been satisfactorily resolved, it is important to realise that in Egypt there existed an intellectual climate that favoured an ancient tradition which had survived centuries of foreign occupation.

To some extent this phenomenon was encouraged by the belief in the imminent end of the world and in the near approach of the second coming. The corruptions of the world were rejected, in favour of the search for god in solitude.

According to tradition Egyptian monasticism was founded by Paul of Thebes (who died around 341). He is said to have lived in a fashion that bordered on the miraculous, in a cave near the Red Sea. His meeting in old age with Saint Anthony furnished Coptic piety with a famous image. Saint Anthony is a less mythical figure: his life, recorded in 356 by Saint Athanasius, bishop of Alexandria, showed the strength of self-denial and solitude. Egyptian monasticism was organised by Saint Pachomius (286-348). He was twenty years old before he became a Christian. His early training in the Egyptian literary tradition had a profound effect upon him; this is seen in the Pachomian Rule. His division of the monastic communities, first into "families" and then into "houses" of monks who followed similar occupations, recalls the structure of the ancient Egyptian priesthood. Of the forty characteristics of the ideal monastic leader, twenty were drawn from the Bible and twenty from the pharaonic tradition; they were expressed in a gnomic form which recalls the Book of the Dead. That Saint Pachomius should have remained faithful to the old Egyptian books of wisdom shows the reputation they had retained. It was also perhaps meant to confirm the Egyptian character of the movement.

From Egypt the Pachomian Rule spread to the west through the work of Saint Athanasius (299-373), who took refuge in Rome from 340 to 346. His life of Saint Anthony paved the way for the dissemination of monastic institutions to Syria, Cappadocia and Greece. Through its influence on the Rule of Saint Basil, and hence, indirectly, on that of Saint Benedict, the Egyptian movement was the source of both eastern and western monasticism, and contributed decisively to the moral and social force of Christianity. Men of all walks of life came to follow the teachings and imitate the example of the Egyptian ascetics.

These solitary holy men, luminaries of the spiritual life, attracted pilgrims from all over the world, making Egypt a new Holy Land. This reputation enabled the patriarchs of Alexandria to constitute themselves champions of orthodoxy. They maintained a merciless battle against heresy. Athanasius, with the assistance of Anthony and Pachomius, was celebrated for his fight against Arianism. This heresy, condemned at the Council of Nicaea, denied the consubstantiality of the Trinity and, in consequence, the divinity of Christ. A century later Cyril of Alexandria wrestled with equal vigour against the Nestorian heresy. This questioned Mary's right to the title of Mother of God, and the doctrine of the unity of the word made faith.

Egypt at this time enjoyed huge prestige throughout the Christian world; she was "the sanctuary of orthodoxy . . . land of faith . . . the home of monks." Pilgrims came, not to see the famous tombs or the biblical sites, but to venerate the "Living Saints."

Meanwhile, with the aid of fanatics and an army of devout monks, the patriarchs of Alexandria fought an unremitting battle against paganism.

Rivalry with Byzantium

The growing influence of the patriarchate of Constantinople, strategically placed at the heart of the empire, began to rival that of Alexandria, then at the height of its power and aspiring to found an Alexandrian papacy. The bishop of Alexandria took the title of pope in the east. Egyptian nationalism supported the Egyptian church; it was seen as the successor of the pharaohs. Like the pharaohs it was rich, thanks to its monopolies of funerals and of trade in nitre, papyrus and salt.

In 381 the ecumenical Council of Constantinople gave to Constantinople the precedence, after Rome, that had previously been accorded to Alexandria. This decision, though never recognised in Egypt or the rest of the East, exacerbated the rivalry. The Egyptian patriarch Theophilus humiliated and crushed his Byzantine rival Saint John Chrysostom, following his quarrel with Egyptian Origenist monks. His nephew Cyril (376-444) caused Nestorius, patriarch of Constantinople, to be condemned and deposed at the Council of Ephesus in 431. Cyril's successor, Dioscuros, supported Eutyches, archimandrite of the monastery of Constantinople, a proponent of monophysitism. This doctrine refused to recognise the dual nature of Christ, maintaining that his humanity was absorbed by his divinity, "dissolved like a drop of honey in the sea." Eutyches had been deposed by his bishop Flavian, but Dioscuros, at a further council at Ephesus in 449, secured his re-instatement and the deposition of Flavian. Dioscuros assumed the title of ecumenical patriarch; his see resembled a new Rome. However, the very excess of his triumph brought about his downfall.

Chalcedon and schism

Alexandria's former allies united against her. Pope Leo, formerly her supporter, persuaded the emperor Marcian to summon a council to Chalcedon in 451. Monophysitism was declared heretical and Dioscuros deposed. The quarrel was one of words rather than beliefs; the Council insisted that Christ had a two-fold nature, both human and divine; the monophysites insisted that he had a single nature, with dual aspects. Dioscuros, stripped of his ministry, refused to submit; he was exiled, and died in 454. The Egyptian people refused to accept the decision of Chalcedon. Alexandrian rejection of the new bishop was answered by persecutions; they failed to secure peace. For nearly two centuries monophysitism became the symbol of national resistance. The emperor Justinian instituted a reign of terror, giving the patriarch Paul extraordinary powers to discipline the recalcitrant. Monophysite churches were closed; their members were barred from public office and professional posts. Paul's successor Apollinaris adopted bloody methods, which did not succeed in forcing the Alexandrians to submit. His butchery (200,000 killed) brought only apparent calm. Justinian himself destroyed the administrative unity of the country to control it better and to facilitate the raising of taxes. Severe penalties were imposed on those who evaded taxation. Many abandoned their land and took to the desert.

Under Justinian's more tolerant successors the monophysite patriarchate was restored. Its former strength was renewed by the energetic Damian (518-604); after reconciliation with Antioch it reached the height of its power.

The Egyptians, liberated momentarily from the Byzantine yoke by the Persians (619-629), suffered renewed persecutions under Heraclius, the exarch of Africa who had revolted and declared himself emperor. He replaced the Coptic patriarch Benjamin with Cyrus of Colchis. Six years of terror followed, its perpetrator surviving in popular memory as the first manifestation of the anti-Christ. Neither torture nor exile, nor all the other excesses of the "Caucasian," could quell the spirit of monophysitism. The break between the church of Alexandria and the other Christian churches, which followed the Council of Chalcedon, converted it to a national church with deeply rooted traditions; these have remained almost unchanged to the present day. Its isolation was increased by the Arab conquest.

The Arab conquest

The disorganisation and fragmentation of the Byzantine army, and the Egyptian hatred of the imperial occupier, together explain the feeble resistance offered in 639, to Amr Ibn al-As, the general of Caliph Omar. Cyrus, who had presently fallen into disfavour due to some obscure dealings with the enemy, was sent back to Alexandria after the death of Heraclius with orders to secure peace with the Arabs and to negotiate a government acceptable to the Egyptians. He was well received by Amr and signed a treaty in 641. For the eleven months of armistice Egypt was to pay a tribute; the Muslims undertook to respect Christian churches and not to interfere in their affairs. Many Egyptians believed that the Roman defeat was retribution for the tyranny of Heraclius, and for the persecutions inflicted through his instrument Cyrus. They believed also that the conquering Bedouins would soon return to the desert with the tribute and plunder they had won.

At first the Copts had little complaint against their new masters. Amr recalled the exiled bishops, re-instated the Alexandrian patriarch Benjamin, respected church property and restored to the monophysites the churches confiscated by the melchites. Government of the country was entrusted to the Copts.

This liberal treatment did not last. As the Arab empire grew the caliphs burdened the country with a taxation as crippling as that of Byzantium had been. Harassment and persecution followed: the government was placed in Arab hands, religious symbols were burned, vestments forbidden, churches and monasteries destroyed and property confiscated. Rebellions were ruthlessly suppressed. Many Copts were converted to Islam; the poor to escape taxation, the ambitious to gain positions of power. These afflictions began under the Fatimid caliph, al-Hakim, an unbalanced and cruel ruler who confiscated church property and destroyed a number of places of worship; he forbade processions and imposed restrictions on dress. But it was above all the Mamelukes who dealt most cruelly with the Egyptian Christians. They burned and pillaged monasteries and churches (fifty-nine in the reign of al-Malik al-Nasir alone according to the chronicler al-Maqrizi). Massacres occurred during disturbances created by agents provocateurs. Christians were forbidden to ride horses or to hold government posts; they were obliged to wear a blue turban and bells about their neck before entering a bath. During this period (1250-1517) the Christian community was ruined; by the nineteenth century it formed only a tenth of the total population of Egypt.

As the Arab regime converted from a temporary military occupation to permanent colonisation the use of the Coptic language began to decline. In 706 Arabic was declared the official language of government. As a result the language of the country was progressively suppressed; by the end of the tenth century it was spoken only by a minority. The liturgy was translated into Arabic by the patriarch Gabriel II (1132-1145). The latest known Coptic manuscripts date from the end of the fourteenth century. The necessities of trade effectively compelled the Copts to adopt the language and writing of their conquerors. With each generation the Coptic tongue lost ground, until it survived only in the services of the church.

The legacy of the past

The philosophical tradition of Egyptian paganism, which was still alive in the Egyptian mentality, found in Christianity a response to many of its aspirations: its ideal of purity, its concern with the world to come, with judgement after death and a paradise beyond the grave. In the Christian climate it was more at ease than with the Graeco-Egyptian tradition. This legacy from the past profoundly influenced Egyptian Christianity; the latter adapted the ancient symbols, images and forms of worship to express its own vision of Christ, conformable to the genius of its people. A few examples will make this clear.

The Copts saw no necessity to alter the Egyptian calendar. They retained the names of the months which had commemorated the pharaonic gods and festivals. The Coptic new year was the first day of the month of Thoth, corresponding to the 29th of August of the Julian calendar. Faithful to tradition, the Copts divided the year into the three seasons of flood, seedtime and harvest; to each they consecrated prayers of intercession in the course of the mass. Towards the end of the fourth century the Copts adopted, as symbol of their church, the hieroglyph denoting life or *ankh*, held by the ancient divinities; a form of Christian cross widely current at the time had a short upper arm, surmounted, in sign of triumph by a circular crown, the whole strangely resembling the Egyptian hieroglyph. In consciously adopting it, the Egyptian Christians wished to demonstrate to their pagan brethren that their gods had heralded and advocated Christianity.

One of the oldest elements of Egyptian belief, deriving from the Old Kingdom, is the divine judgement that awaits the soul. Its very antiquity recommended it to the early Christians. This explains, in Coptic eschatology, the belief in a "book," a sort of register in which were written all man's deeds, both good and bad. It explains especially the weighing of souls by Saint Michael before the celestial tribunal; the role of Thoth naturally devolved upon the first and most popular of the archangels.

More important is the influence of Egyptian thought on a crucial point of Christian theology: the nature of Christ as son of God. What can have been the origin of the concept, so extraordinary at first sight, of a man god who was also a king? The idea of the king as a son of god had been for thousands of years a tenet of Egyptian theology. This was well known to orthodox Judaism; such knowledge must have favoured a disposition towards such a belief among Christians. It was a Jew, Paul of Tarsus, who was the first to develop and propagate these ideas. Origen, the first great theologian of the church, who was a native of Egypt, clearly propounded the divine nature of the man Jesus.

In these examples we can see how the past moulded Egyptian Christianity and gave it its originality. Its individuality is expressed in the forms and observance which the Copts have zealously preserved, despite numberless difficulties, as the surest guarantee of their identity.

Egyptian Christians recognise seven sacraments: baptism, confirmation, confession, communion, ordination, marriage and extreme unction. The only recognised form of baptism is total immersion – three times. Periods of fasting and abstinence are remarkable for their length and severity; they account for just over two thirds of the year, during which animal food, including milk, cheese, eggs and butter, is forbidden. This emphasis on fasting is doubtless a legacy of the ancient Egyptian desire for bodily and spiritual purity, and the ascetic excesses of the desert monks.

An art of the people

Coptic art, for a long time little appreciated, is difficult to define; its unity of style is not immediately apparent. Standing between the two great periods, the pharaonic and the Islamic, of which so many great works are extant, Coptic art appears at a disadvantage. This does not preclude a considerable artistic achievement; certain works were produced which stand comparison with the master works of more glittering periods. Today it is very much appreciated in certain western cities, which value its non-conformist attitude; its total freedom is in sympathy with contemporary rejections of established formulae.

The origins of Coptic art go back to the first centuries of Christianity, though it was at first slow to free itself from the influence of contemporary pagan work. It is essentially a popular art – the first of its kind in eastern antiquity. All arts until then had been arts of patronage. Commissions had emanated from the royal courts; artists were trained in workshops, where they were taught techniques and acquired a repertoire of forms. This method accounts for the unity of style and fine standard of workmanship of the highly wrought artefacts of ancient Egypt and Mesopotamia, aristocratic arts par excellence. This perfection of forms had a negative concomitant: an absence of inner life and of the spontaneous creativity which characterises popular art.

Alienated by political and religious differences, the only official building that Byzantium bestowed on Egypt was the fourth century basilica of Saint Menas in Alexandria. It was built by Byzantine artists who had no sympathy with Egyptian taste. It had no influence or imitators. The Egyptian church was left to its own resources: serving no political power, it was free from official restrictions. The church's artists drew their inspiration whence they wished, with total freedom of expression and with an absence of regimentation. Improvisation, and unexpected touches of inventive genius springing from the collective imagination of the people, give this style a peculiar charm.

A predominant characteristic of Coptic art lies in its ornamentation of surfaces. The motifs, derived from earlier periods, had largely lost both their meaning and function. They were used for their own sake with an astonishing sense of decorative composition.

Another trait which gives Coptic art its originality is its mastery of stylisation. The innovative genius of the Coptic artists converted the traditional motifs of their predecessors into an almost abstract art; foliage scrolls became geometric patterns which anticipated the arabesques of Muslim art.

Following the period of Alexander the Great, Hellenistic art and its later heir, Roman art, came to supplant the indigenous arts throughout the east. But though Alexandria became strongly Hellenised the rest of Egypt was only superficially so; popular traditions were submerged but not destroyed. It was in these inland regions that Coptic art developed. Its repertoire was at first largely Graeco-Roman: mythological scenes, winged victories, cupids, acanthus leaves and vine branches – decorative themes derived from Roman sarcophagi and mosaics. Some themes received a Christian interpretation; the very popular vine branches of Dionysius became the emblem of the church – the vine of the Lord. But this Graeco-Roman art did not fully satisfy the Coptic artists; they wished to free themselves of things Greek as a symbol of their national rejection of the Byzantine yoke.

The removal of the imperial capital to Constantinople in 330 transferred the sphere of influence further east, stimulating a return to oriental sources of inspiration. Artists turned their attention to Asia, where lay the native land of Christ, and took as models the sculpture of Palmyra and Syria and the silks and metalwork of Persia. Thus Sassanian works played a formative role in the development of Coptic art.

Under these influences Coptic artists produced unusual and inventive work in many fields – in architecture, in ornamental carving in wood and stone, in painting and in the decorative arts. Certain of their achievements are of the highest quality; the tapestries in coloured wool and the foliate tracery of the sixth century monastic churches are pure masterpieces.

A religious architecture

The surviving Christian monuments of this age give only a feeble idea of the incredible upsurge of building which covered the whole country. Monasteries and churches were so numerous in the deserts that it was said that the traveller never lost sight of one by day or night.

The early Christians destroyed pagan shrines and adapted tombs and temples to the new belief. But a new architecture was rapidly evolved. The Coptic artists broke with pharaonic art, associated in their eyes with paganism; yet, consciously or not, they borrowed many of its forms. The cubic shapes and inclined walls of their convents and monastic churches strangely recall the temples of ancient Egypt. The churches of the Red and the White monasteries in Middle Egypt, built in the mid fifth century, are the oldest surviving monuments of this period. They are basilican in plan, with a trefoil apse surmounted by a wooden roof with exposed beams; the last has long disappeared. Within, two rows of columns form a nave and side aisles with two tiers of Corinthian columns; they frame niches with sculpted frontals and uprights.

A sculpture of ornament

Coptic sculpture was at its finest in the sixth and seventh centuries; it is, with tapestries, the art in which the Coptic spirit found its finest expression. It is above all a sculpture of ornament. Statuary was treated with reserve, if not with suspicion.

Ornamental infilling, inherited from Ptolemaic art, was widely used. It appears on the shafts of columns, on lintels, friezes and capitals. Graeco-Roman motifs were transformed by a sense of decorative composition proper to the Coptic genius. The naturalistic plant forms of Roman sculpture, which stood out clearly on a light ground, were abandoned in favour of an imaginary vegetation which became flattened and simplified to the point of geometrical abstraction – without, however, becoming in any way arid.

The capitals, mostly Corinthian, are formed of three tiers of acanthus. Coptic stylisation transformed the full soft leaf into one with deeply lacinated lobes, with triple dentations. Interlaced with volutes and tracery, its elements make up vigorous geometric designs. Other types of capital occur: inverted cones whose surfaces are covered with flat decoration, capitals with vine leaves, corbel capitals . . .

An art that pleases and instructs

Coptic painting is little known. That which remains in the monasteries is difficult to date, due to frequent repainting and restoration over the centuries. The oldest mention of the figurative painting of the Copts comes from Arab writers: they were much struck by the originality and beauty of the figures, doubtless because human representations did not exist in their art.

The Copts greatly emphasised painting in their buildings, considering it a medium both educational and decorative. Their general rule in painting a sacred building was to decorate the apse with figurative representations; the most visible and holy place, it enclosed the altar or the tomb of a martyr. Pillars and columns, admirably suited to the portrayal of standing figures, were particularly favoured. A unique success was achieved with the fresco. The early style still shows Hellenistic or post-classical influences, and usually represents historical themes, often with floral or geometric decoration. Later, though still influenced by Hellenistic formulae in the use of animal decoration and allegorical figures, the fresco assumed a monumental character, combined with ornamental forms. Niche frontals, covered with geometric motifs, circles or lozenges enclosing fruit, flowers, birds, sometimes portraits or allegorical figures, are surmounted by representations of the prophets, the saints or the Virgin; Christ is often represented, surrounded by the symbols of the Apocalypse.

Hellenistic portraiture, which had spread from Alexandria throughout the Mediterranean was one of the primary influences on painting in its beginnings and gave birth to the icon. In the rare surviving specimens one sees the same characteristics, the huge eyes and expression of grave concentration.

Tapestries: a summit of achievement

Since antiquity Egypt had excelled in weaving. This is the most famous and esteemed aspect of Coptic art. The basic materials were linen and wool. Silk, introduced under the Ptolemies, became one of the most important Alexandrian products. Its use, strictly controlled under the Romans because of its price and the difficulty of producing it, was limited to the imperial palace. Linen was used in its natural colour especially in Lower Egypt. Woolen fabrics were a speciality of Upper Egypt. Tunics were decorated with bands around the neck and on each side of the chest; the motifs, in coloured wool, were woven in gobelin stitch. At first these were one with the fabric; later they were made separately and applied. Their inspiration came from three sources: Hellenistic, oriental and Christian. This last enriched the repertoire by introducing scenes from the Old and the New Testament. Free from official controls and subject only to their own inspiration, the Coptic artists gave full rein to their imagination.

From the third to the fifth century mythological figures predominate: putti, dancers, nereids riding sea monsters, or decorative themes forming geometrical or floral shapes among which are inserted gazelles, lions, hares, birds and small figures.

The sixth century is a transitional period, without distinct character. With the official adoption of Christianity throughout the empire Christian elements became pronounced; pagan themes received a Christian interpretation; crosses appeared. In the seventh and eighth centuries the true characteristics of Coptic art are apparent; shapes became simple, sometimes to the point of caricature; the tendency towards abstraction was accentuated. But the fragments which have survived are difficult to date exactly since the different styles spread to the many textile centres in the country in varying degrees.

Towards the ninth century the Islamic prohibition against any representation of the human figure obliged the Coptic weavers to modify their designs.

93

91. Mount Saint Catherine, in the Sinai peninsula. The steps were carved by the monks of the monastery.

92. A stretch of desert in the Sinai near the sea, with pools of salt water.

93. The monastery of Saint Anthony, founded in the third century AD. Christians fled to the desert not only to escape persecution and the heavy taxes imposed by Byzantium.
There was also a conscious desire to establish a new form of devotion: withdrawal from everyday life to hermitages, convents and monasteries, far from cities and worldly life. It is not by accident that the first monasteries were founded in Egypt since already during pharaonic times we find evidence of people retiring from the world in order to communicate better with Amon-Re and other gods.

94. Coptic funerary stele. Vatican, Egyptian Museum.

95. The Greek Orthodox cross on a wall of the monastery of Saint Catherine.

96. Detail of the interior of the church dedicated to Saint Barbara, in the old city-centre of Cairo.

97-98. The monastery of Saint Anthony. The complex of churches, chapels, living quarters and gardens is surrounded by an imposing defence wall, in some places twelve metres high. Some of the chapels still have frescoes of subjects very characteristic of Christian Egypt: anchorites and warrior saints, in particular Michael and Gabriel.

94

95

97

96

99

99. Coptic tapestry. Paris, Louvre. The finest art form of the Copts was undoubtedly tapestry weaving; they used linen and wool since silk could be used only for the imperial palace.

100

)1

100. The monastery of Saint Paul on the Red Sea. According to tradition, Egyptian monasticism was founded by Paul of Thebes, who died around 341 AD.

101. Coptic fresco of a warrior saint.

102

103

102-104. The Christian monastery of Deir Amba Baramus, in the Wadi Natrun area.

Islamic Egypt

The Arab conquest

Egypt was conquered by the Arabs between 639 and 642. Exasperated by the tyranny of the Byzantines, the people accepted the agreement that followed the fall of the Roman and Byzantine fortress of Babylon (the terms included an eleven-month truce and a heavy tax on the practice of Christianity) with indifference and even relief. No one suspected that the new civilisation would break radically with the old traditions. The Egyptians initially had few grounds for complaint. The new potentate, Amr, reinstated the Coptic patriarch Benjamin at Alexandria and respected Church property. He recalled the exiled bishops and returned to the Monophysites the churches that had been turned over to the Melchites. He allowed Copts who held public office to retain their positions, and he conferred new offices on others. He moved the administrative centre of the country from Alexandria toward the south of the delta, where he established a new capital, al-Fustat. But this initial liberalism diminished as the Arab Empire expanded: administered from Medina, Damascus, or Baghdad, Egypt became a mere province which developed within the limits imposed by prefects of the caliphate who aspired solely to accumulate the greatest wealth in the briefest time possible, and to send the caliph conspicuous revenues. Spurred by economic pressures, the process of Islamisation became increasingly rapid after 717.

The Copts did not readily accept the Arab domination, which for them now meant fiscal oppression and the confiscation or destruction of their churches. Their endeavours to evade the capitation tax led to violence and bloodshed. The ordinance promulgated in 706 by the prefect Abdullah Ibn Abdel Malik, according to which all official documents had to be written in Arabic, dealt a fatal blow to the Coptic language. The need to maintain trade relations with their countrymen forced the Copts to learn the Arabic language and alphabet. The Coptic language held out for a few centuries and then disappeared from daily life, although it continued to be used in religious contexts. Meanwhile the Arab Empire, having become too large, began to decentralise. Egypt benefited from this process, reacquiring a certain degree of political independence under the aegis of local dynasties.

TULUNIDS AND IKSHIDITES (868-968)

A certain autonomy

The first of the new dynasts, Ahmed Ibn Tulun, a Turkish chief vested with unlimited powers, was sent in 868 to re-establish order in the troubled province of Egypt. He took advantage of his mandate to break away from the empire of Baghdad and re-establish an independent dynasty on the banks of the Nile.

Refined, literate and clear-sighted, he set about reviving the country's ruined economy. His judicious administration – characterised by improved finances, tax reform and strict surveillance of functionaries – succeeded in restoring prosperity. The considerable income which lay at his disposal enabled him to embellish al-Katai, the new suburb of al-Fustat, and to build one of the most beautiful and famous mosques in Egypt.

He restored the border fortifications to a state of efficiency and maintained a formidable fleet and army. In 878 he conquered Syria except for Antioch, where he took refuge until his death in May 884 following a rebellion in his army. His son Khumaruya, who ascended the throne at the age of twenty, had a weakness for lavish display and gracious living. His unlimited extravagance irritated Baghdad, which was deprived of important revenues and feared his bad example. The Abbasids acted firmly and brutally in 905, ending the dynasty, destroying the town built by Ibn Tulun, sacking al-Fustat, and re-establishing their authority on the banks of the Nile. But their triumph was short-lived.

In 935 the Ikshid Mohammed Ibn Tughj, who had come to restore order, assumed control of the country. The dynasty that he founded (939-68) is known chiefly for having repelled the Fatimids, who sailed for Egypt from North Africa. After his death in 946, an Abyssinian eunuch, Kafur, came to power and ascended the throne in 965, at the extinction of the dynasty. A patron of the arts and lover of pleasure, he held a sumptuous court frequented by scholars, poets and musicians. At his death in 968 the country was considerably debilitated, and its economy was disorganised.

THE FATIMID ANTICALIPHATE (969-1171)

Independence

Al-Muizz, the fourth caliph of a new schismatic power that arose in North Africa – the Fatimids – had one ambition, namely, to rule over the wealthy land of Egypt and its peaceful people. Circumstances were in his favour, as the Arab Empire had been shaken by Carmathian terrorist raids on Baghdad and there was chaos in Egypt following the death of Kafur and the terrible famine of 967. Al-Muizz sent his minister Jauhar at the head of a formidable army to conquer the Nile valley in 969, which Jauhar did without encountering resistance. Breaking all ties with the Abbasid Empire, Egypt immediately became an independent kingdom. Orthodox Sunnism was officially replaced by the schismatic faith of the Shiites as a new caliphate rivalling that of Baghdad took charge of religious life. The great majority of the populace, however, remained faithful to the orthodox doctrine; those who converted were compelled to do so by poverty or hunger.

Jauhar re-established order and let Egyptians hold office in his government. At the beginning of his reign he founded a new capital, al-Kahira ("The Victorious" – Cairo) north of al-Fustat, which he built in the record time of two years. Al-Muizz ascended the throne of Egypt in 974 amid great festivities and sumptuous ceremonies. He erected the mosque of al-Azhar (the beauty of which was to be unequalled), as well as other important monuments, in the area surrounding his palace. He reformed the judiciary system, the basis of property tax and the collection of tributes to produce an enormous income; this in turn he spent on maintaining a highly efficient army and a fleet of more than six hundred ships. Despite his judicious reign, however, trouble broke out between Sunnites and Shiites, and a Carmath raid reached the gates of Cairo in 971. The Fatimids succeeded from time to time in obtaining a nominal allegiance of the holy cities of Arabia.

The moderate and liberal al-Aziz, who succeeded al-Muizz in 975, encouraged religious dialogue between Copts and Muslims and treated Jews and Christians unusually well in his government, in order to counterbalance the influence of the Sunnites.

His successor, al-Hakim, who ascended the throne at the age of eleven, indulged in such extravagances that many considered him mad. He proclaimed himself god and found followers who believed in his divinity, including a certain Daran, who emigrated to Syria to preach his cult. After al-Hakim's mysterious disappearance, the sect of the Druses (whose name derives from Daran) preached his return. Under his reign the persecution of Jews and Christians, which had become quite common, was extended to orthodox Muslims.

After a promising start the Fatimids fell victim to their love of pleasure and incredible luxury; they delegated their power to their viziers. Their legitimacy was questioned by the theologians, and their control of government was assured solely by their legions, recruited chiefly in North Africa. They levied taxes arbitrarily, and the rivalries between Turkish and black regiments degenerated into revolts, riots and assassinations which made matters even worse and led, among other things, to the destruction of the artistic treasures and the library of the caliphs. The longest reign, that of al-Mustansir (1036-94), was marred by a prolonged famine of frightening intensity, during which the populace is believed to have resorted to anthropophagy. The governor of Acre, Badr al-Jamali, restored order and massacred the Turkish Guard in 1073. He surrounded Cairo with a formidable stone wall with three monumental gates flanked by bastions that doubled as prisons.

Meanwhile two serious threats had appeared on the horizon. On one hand the Seldjukid Turks, whose power had developed dangerously, had begun to advance towards Egypt, occupying Persia and part of Syria. On the other the crusaders, favoured by factional strife among the Islamic nations, had conquered Palestine and Jerusalem. The caliphs of Cairo considered the latter threat the less worrisome, if not for Egypt at least for their own dynasty.

SALADIN AND THE AYYUBITE EMPIRE (1169-1250)

When King Amaury I of Jerusalem invaded their territory the Fatimids appealed for aid to the Syrians. Shirkub's army succeeded in saving the Egyptian dynasty. Following his death in 1169, his nephew Salah al-Din Yussuf Ibn Ayyub (Saladin) was nominated vizier. By skilfully manoeuvring between the Shiite caliph of Cairo and the Sunnite prince of Damascus, Saladin managed to free himself of both of them and found an independent monarchy. He began by suppressing a revolt of the Sudanese Guard and repelling an attack by the Byzantine emperor and the king of Jerusalem against Damietta. A victorious campaign in Palestine consolidated his popularity. In an effort to gain the people's support he fomented a religious revolution, having the name of the caliph suppressed during the Friday prayers, following the latter's death in 1171. At this time one of the most glorious reigns in the Muslim history of Egypt began.

Saladin's first concern was to re-establish Sunnism. This he achieved by creating unified teaching centres, the "madrasas," to train devoted masters and obedient functionaries. He consolidated his power by constructing a citadel on the Mokattam plateau which dominated the four cities, al-Fustat, al-Katai, al-Askar and al-Kahira. He made peace in the country up to the Sudan, and he conquered Yemen. Following the death in 1174 of Nasr al-Din, king of Damascus and Saladin's former mentor, the latter deployed the combined military resources of the Islamic nations against the crusaders. His Syrian campaign of 1174-75 gave him control over the south of the country. Bitterly defeated by the Franks in 1177, he beat them back from the walls of Damascus two years later after having unified his command and occupied all of Syria (up to Aleppo). In 1182 his occupied territories were extended to include part of Upper Mesopotamia. The Frankish forces ventured an expedition on Medina, but were captured, and several prisoners were beheaded at Mecca on the Day of Sacrifices.

The great offensive of the holy war began in 1187 and lasted fifteen months. Saladin seized Tiberiad, Saint Jean d'Acre and numerous other strongholds; and he occupied Jerusalem. Although he had defeated the reign of the crusaders, he was unable to proceed further because of insurmountable financial difficulties, the low morale of his officers and his lack of a fleet. The treaty of Ramleh of 1191 was fairly advantageous for the Muslims. The crusaders kept only the coastal towns between Jaffa and Antioch and reserved the right to visit Jerusalem. The Muslims won access to the ports and began to trade profitably with Europe.

Having united the Muslims and expelled the Christians from the Holy City, Saladin enjoyed unequalled prestige. He died in 1193, leaving his heirs the broadest empire that had ever been governed by Cairo, ranging from Egypt to Yemen, Syria and Mesopotamia, up to the Euphrates. This legacy would be partially compromised later. The government of the different provinces was entrusted to his sons and brothers, whose envy and ambition generated a tangle of alliances and fratricidal wars which ended with the rise to power of the king's brother Malik Adil (1200-18), whose firm rule and diplomacy managed to safeguard the bases of Saladin's empire. The crusaders were torn by similar rivalries; despite a situation that was favourable to their cause, they attempted one attack only, against Damietta, in 1218. While they laid siege to the city Malik Adil, on his way to Syria, died suddenly and was succeeded by his son Malik Kamil. The crusaders took Damietta in November 1219 and closed in on the capital; but, harassed by the king's troops, they unconditionally surrendered. The eight-year truce that ensued was turned to advantage by the Syrians, who fomented disorders and isolated Malik Kamil diplomatically (the latter secretly delivered Jerusalem to Frederick II on 17 March 1229 in exchange for the promise to defend Egypt from all aggression). The king launched a stout offensive against the princes of Syria and Mesopotamia who had leagued against him, and he took Damascus. He died on 9 March 1238 as a new, dynamic and formidable power – Turkey – appeared on the horizon.

After the death of Malik Kamil the factional strife between princes broke out with renewed fervour. Malik Salih occupied the throne of Egypt when the seventh crusade, commanded by Louis IX of France, reached Damietta (5 June 1249). Overcome by panic, the Egyptian troops retreated to Mansura where Salih died on 23 November 1249. The French were defeated by the king's Mameluke Guard commanded by the queen, Shajar al-Durr, a bold and forcible woman who kept the king's death secret and preserved unity until the arrival of the heir to the throne. Dissatisfied with the conduct of the latter, the Mamelukes assassinated him and offered the throne to Shajar al-Durr, who became "Malikat al-Muslimin" (Queen of the Muslims), the only woman to occupy the throne of Egypt in the Islamic era.

Opposed by the Syrian emirs, her monarchy officially lasted eighty days; but her marriage to the commander-in-chief of her army (who was appointed sultan) permitted her to do as she wished while he was away quelling revolts. She eventually had him murdered, but in the end was herself killed by rivals in his harem.

Egypt prospered under the Ayyubites. Agriculture and trade flourished, and as a result of its felicitous geographical position the country became a point of contact between the East, the Far East and Europe. This status brought considerable advantages.

THE MAMELUKE SULTANS (1250-1517)

Daring parvenus

The term Mameluke ("belonging to") designates the mercenary slaves who were recruited as soldiers of the emirs and formed their guard corps. Circassian, Greek, Turkish, Albanian or Serbo-Croatian by birth, they were purchased as adolescents and trained for one end only – courage in battle. Street fights, conspiracies, raids on bazaars and public baths to procure women: their animated life was characterised by boldness and spirit of initiative. Their status as slaves released them from all moral obligation and gave them unlimited freedom of action.

The Mameluke rulers of Egypt can be divided into two groups according to their origin: the Turkish Bahri (1250-1381), so called because of the cantonment of their elite corps on the isle of Roda on the river (Bahr); and the Circassians (1382-1517), advocates of the suppression of hereditary power.

The murder of Turan-Shah, the last of the Ayyubites, was instigated and perpetrated chiefly by a Turkish Mameluke named Bibars, who had belonged to the king's father. Bibars was to wait some ten years before ascending the throne. He reigned for sixteen years, during which time he brought Egypt a victory even more decisive than that of Saladin over the crusaders. In less than twenty years he and his successors Kalaun and Malik Ashraf Khalil freed Palestine, took Saint Jean d'Acre (1291), Sidon and Beirut, thus bringing an end to the crusades.

After the Mongolian invasion of Syria and the fall of the caliphate of Baghdad (in 1258), the heir of the last Abbasid caliph took refuge at Cairo. Bibars acknowledged him as the spiritual leader of Islam and received in exchange the temporal powers of the caliph as "defender of the faith." The presence of the caliph at Cairo brought increased prestige to Egypt.

Bibars won back Syria, repelled the Mongols, had himself proclaimed sultan and organised the first great Muslim military empire. The administrative machinery that he constructed remained intact until the Ottoman conquest. He built roads, canals and dams, and established a relay-postal system, an army and a fleet, bringing Egypt to the peak of its power. He defeated the Mongols again in 1277, but died in the same year of a poison he had prepared for another.

The aged general Kalaun (1279-89) was elected sultan following a brief interlude. After defeating the Mongols at Homs in 1281, he obtained a seventeen-year truce. He was succeeded by his son Mohammed Ibn Kalaun, who ruled in peace for thirty years, governing the country with a firm hand, through the mediation of military officers to whom the clerks of state, entrusted with the collection of taxes, were directly responsible.

The Mamelukes, like their predecessors the Ayyubites, realised the importance of trading with Europe, India and China. They signed treaties with the Genoese, the Catalans, the Pisans, the Marseillais and the Venetians, whose merchant marines called at Alexandria for oriental goods, especially spices; and from whom the Egyptians obtained the raw materials they lacked, such as iron and wood. These highly lucrative commercial exchanges brought considerable prosperity for Muslim merchants. The Christians, however, were excluded.

The continuous conflicts among the emirs, the demand for silver, and growing insecurity generated repeated revolts. These were bloodily suppressed; violence reigned freely for about forty years, accompanied by a slackening of morals.

The Circassian Barkuk seized power in 1382 and restored order. Thanks to this new dynasty Egypt escaped the invasion of Tamerlane, who decimated West Asia after 1393; and conquered Cyprus in 1428. But the fifteenth century was dominated by continuous street-fighting at Cairo. Fiscal policy followed the whim of the bureaucracy, and the upper classes replaced free trade with a monopoly that enabled them to sell food products at high prices. Intellectual and artistic life, in contrast, developed remarkably, and Cairo became the spiritual and religious capital of Islam. The magnificent court of the sultans and their generous patronage (expressed in the building of mosques, tombs, schools and hospitals) made Cairo much more splendid than Baghdad had been in its finest days.

The reigns of the last Circassians, Kait Bey (1468-96) and Kansuh al-Ghuri (1501-16), despite their magnificence, witnessed the decline of economic prosperity. Vasco de Gama discovered the sea route to India around the Cape of Good Hope in 1498. The Egyptian ports were doomed and the economy ruined. Together with the Venetians, who shared their ill fate, the sultans declared war on the Portuguese; but their fleet was destroyed on 3 February 1509 off Diu.

Selim I, sultan of Constantinople, after conquering the Persians, defeated and killed Kansuh al-Ghuri near Aleppo. The Egyptian king was succeeded by his nephew Tumanbey, who organised the resistance against the Turks and met them on 22 January 1517 at Ridanya, a suburb north of Cairo, in a battle of singular violence. Tumanbey was delivered up to the sultan by treachery and hung from the Zuwela gate on 12 April 1517. The last caliph was taken away to Constantinople.

THE OTTOMAN OCCUPATION (1517-1798)

The dark centuries

Impoverished and weakened, Egypt diminished in economic and cultural importance. The Turks ruled with the collaboration of the Mamelukes, reduced to the status of mere beys. To forestall rebellion, power was divided between a governor appointed by the Porte, the Pasha of Egypt, and a "divan" (council) of twenty-four Mamelukes. The latter, who were responsible for the collection of taxes, took advantage of their position to sap the country and increase their personal wealth with the heavy tribute due to the sultan. The admirable irrigation system crumbled for lack of maintenance, leading to the ruin of Egyptian agriculture.

The populace abandoned the country, the arable land diminished, and poverty reigned supreme, feeding the fires of disorder and anarchy. The weakening of the Ottoman Empire in the seventeenth and especially the eighteenth century led to that of the pashas of Egypt as well. The Mamelukes took formal possession of the power already tacitly held by their two principal leaders, the "Sheikh el balad" and the "Emir el Hajj." The country entered a period of civil wars during which intrigue and murder triumphed. The Mameluke chief Ali Bey (1757-72) became Sheikh el balad and attempted to break away from Turkish rule; he ceased payment of tribute, coined his own money, and joined forces with the Russians against the Turks. He restored order and conquered Syria. But he was betrayed by his son-in-law and chief lieutenant, and he died before Russian reinforcements could arrive. Egypt again fell into anarchy, exhausted by civil strife and the squandering of its resources.

Egyptian Islam

An essential ingredient of the Egyptian national identity, Islam has played a major part in shaping the country's language, religious customs and architecture. The pride of belonging to the "Umma" (the Community of True Believers) goes hand in hand for most Egyptians with the consciousness of their country's special position among Islamic nations.

Although Islam embraces very different realities, it stands on a basic body of beliefs to which all Muslims subscribe: the absolute oneness of God, religion willed by God after the creation, the one Truth. This gift was revealed to humanity by a series of inspired prophets (from whose teachings Judaism and Christianity also arose, each in the context of its own environment). But because these revelations were corrupted, God addressed a final message to mankind through Mohammed who was the "seal of the prophets" (that is, the last of the series), in the form of the texts that make up the Koran. Diverse political, legal, cultural and mystical tendencies have grown up on the basis of these texts.

Except during the Fatimid period, Egypt has always adhered to Sunnism, the orthodox doctrine followed by the majority of Muslims (as opposed to the Shiites, or followers of Ali, the Prophet's son-in-law, whose adepts are divided into numerous sects found chiefly in Lebanon, Syria, Iraq and Iran). The Koran is the basis of all things for the Sunnites. It is enlightened by the "Sunna," the body of customs and teachings of Mohammed, which explicates the revealed texts. There is no religious hierarchy; instead there are "Ulemas" or Doctors of Islam who study, teach and interpret the revealed law or "sharia." Heirs of the prophets, they come from all social classes.

The mosque of al-Azhar is the traditional focus of religious instruction in Egypt. A place of prayer and of meeting, teaching and assembly, it initially provided studies in the classical Arabic language of the Koran, which students had to learn by heart, and of the "Hadith," accounts of varying length which convey the content of the Sunna. Other disciplines, including theology, Muslim law, the traditions and exegesis of the Koran, were also taught. The teaching method, which resembled indoctrination more than the development of intellectual faculties, rejected all innovation, and eventually became rigid and ineffectual.

The mystical practice of Sufiism, the ultimate goal of which was the union of its adepts with God, developed in Egypt in close association with Azharist culture. Organised in confraternities, each with its own master initiated by a Great Initiator whose lineage led back to the Prophet, the Sufi practised a certain number of devout exercises, the most fundamental of which was the "zikr" or commemoration, the incessant repetition of the name of Allah, aloud and in the heart, singly or in groups, on one or two nights each week. The cult of saints and faith in their intercession, visits to their tombs accompanied by rites of circumambulation, and the celebration of their feast-days, were expressions of piety to which revelry and sexual licence also contributed at times. Sufiism occupied an important place in Egyptian social life. It developed without official support and was sustained only by the generosity of wealthy sympathisers.

The Muslim reformist movement

Egypt is the cradle of the theological movement that attempted to rescue Islam from the Azharist sclerosis and the superstitious practices of Sufiism. During the nineteenth century certain Ulemas took a strong interest in the natural sciences; the concomitant opening up of Egypt to European influence and the pressing need to procure the means of social change shook the educational system violently. But, in addition to offering scientific and material progress, Europe showed disturbing colonial appetites, and many intellectuals were troubled by the intrusion of the West and by the decadence of Muslim culture. They founded a multifarious "reformist" movement that reached well beyond the borders of Egypt and was particularly successful on the home front thanks to the efforts of a zealous Azharist, the sheik Mohammed Abduh (1849-1905). The chief disciple of Jamal al-Din al-Afghani, who preached the revival of

Islam, he came into conflict simultaneously with the "Europeanised" liberal intellectuals and the traditionalist Ulemas. He believed that, in order to revive the spirit of resistance to Europe, it was necessary to purge Islam of the superstitions that marred it, to limit the abuse of polygamy, and to study the human sciences as a means rather than an end. Appointed Grand Mufti of Egypt in 1899, Abduh attempted to reform the Muslim religious courts and to open al-Azhar to the modern world by instituting the "new" subjects of history, geography and mathematics. His chief merit lay in his ability to stimulate resistance against European influence while maintaining the identity of the Islamic countries subject to European colonial rule. His disciples included Qasim Amin (1865-1908), a pioneer of the feminist movement in Egypt who published two works on women's liberation; and Rashid Rida (1865-1935), who became a theoretician of Abduh's theses. The basic idea of Abduh and his followers was to return to true Islam by eliminating the deviations and superstitions which had accumulated down through the ages. The return to the sources – the Koran and the religious traditions of one's "pious ancestors" (al-Salaf al-Salih) – gave the movement the name "Salafiyya," which meant that Islam would become a simple, "rational" religion capable of responding to humanity's every need. The reformists searched unremittingly for a truly Islamic solution "capable of integrating the best of the tradition while selectively accepting those foreign elements that were deemed progressive" (Delanoue). One of their fundamental concerns was the restoration of the literary language, which alone assured continuity with the past and unity with the Umma.

Modern development

The image of the courtyard of al-Azhar packed with pupils seated in a circle around a master and rocking back and forth as they chant verses from the Koran now belongs to the past. Today al-Azhar is a complex of schools and university faculties enlivened by the presence of students and professors from many countries. The course of study was reformed in 1871, 1896 and 1912. During the thirties, the faculties of theology, language and law were organised separately and moved to new buildings. New faculties of business and medicine were created, and the elementary and secondary school curricula were brought into line with those of state schools. A research institute and a library stocked with ancient manuscripts complete the complex. The spiritual heart of Cairo (together with the mosque of al-Hussein where the relics of the Prophet's grandson are preserved), al-Azhar also hosts political assemblies at moments of great national importance.

Muslim culture has another centre, Dar al-Ulum (House of Science), founded in 1882, where modern disciplines are taught to the Azharists who will be responsible for their teaching in the new schools. It is a special faculty of the University of Cairo, accessible both to Azharists and to students from state schools. Together with al-Azhar it produces today's leading religious thinkers and professors of Arabic.

These two centres are unable to respond to all needs. Numerous nomadic schools have been created, and the state universities have sections dedicated to Muslim culture.The first of these universities was founded in 1924, replacing the free university of 1908. Today each major city hosts at least one institution of higher learning. In addition, the Supreme Council of Muslim Affairs, an active organisation endowed with substantial means, founded in 1960, is dedicated to giving concrete reality to Egypt's Islamic vocation. In an enormous publishing endeavour, it has placed the entire heritage of the past at the disposal of scholars. Cairo was the undisputed Arabic book capital until 1950, when it was superceded by Beirut.

Religious instruction is provided for all creeds in the official schools. Teachers of Arabic are also responsible for the religious instruction of Islamic students.

The interpretation of Muslim law and its application to contemporary events are entrusted to an official organism headed by the Grand Mufti.

The Koran occupies a very important place in Egyptian life. Radio and television cover all important religious events, and a special station chants verses of the Koran throughout the day.

The numerous mosques are provided with loudspeakers that call the faithful to prayer at all hours. Friday has become the official day of rest.

Today the various Muslim groups can be divided into two categories. The first includes those who endeavour to create a modern Egypt without reference to religious dogma – the secularists. The other is comprised of those groups which show a pronounced religious tendency – the strongly fundamentalist reformists.

The challenge of fundamentalism

The Confraternity of Muslim Brothers considers itself the true heir of the reformists. Its adherents, no longer satisfied with theory, have turned to action. The founder and supreme leader of this powerful popular movement, which was created in 1928, is Hassan al-Banna. He has organised it in sections commanded by his lieutenants who disseminate his ideology through numerous publications. Retaining from the balanced and clear analyses of the reformists only their hostility toward the West and their desire to return to the Koran, this ideology does not shun recourse to violence (which cost the life of two prime ministers of the monarchy) as a means of achieving their ends. They advocate the segregation of the sexes in social life and in the universities – while wishing to improve the condition of women – as well as the development of cultural and social activities, and the building of hospitals, dispensaries and schools. Since 1945-50, their theoreticians have attempted to draw up a Muslim economic policy, principles of international relations, a concept of social justice of Islamic inspiration, and other practical consequences from an integralist reading of the sharia. Their leading advocate, Sayed Qotb, was hanged by Nasser in 1966. Today the two principal components of the fundamentalist movement are the Muslim Brothers, who follow a moderate line, and a multitude of more or less clandestine associations that do not shy away from the use of violence. Uncontrolled, scattered and little known, they come forth only on such occasions as the attack on the Military Academy in 1974, the assassination of the Minister of Religion in 1977, or in clashes with the Coptic community. Disseminating pamphlets, booklets and sermons, they took control of the Student Union in 1977 at the expense of the Nasserian left. A theatrical and symbolic aspect of the movement is its adoption of Islamic dress: beards and turbans for men, veils for women. The movement's success is largely a result of its social service and self-help programmes. To keep the phenomenon in check,the authorities have prohibited Islamic dress in the universities, increased the police force and taken in hand the administration of social services. The fundamentalists, in turn, have become more prudent, but their influence is no less real. It still pervades the factories, the public administration and the army.

Nasser's socialism and Sadat's liberalism did not produce the prosperity that had been hoped for. As a result, the religious movements have won over the urbanised rural population as well as the middle classes whose sensibilities are offended by social inequality and the inefficiency of the public services.

The Israeli problem has only aggravated the situation. In light of the fear and the void created by the overwhelming victories of Israel in the first three conflicts, the recourse to religious feeling after Israel's example has become common. The first successes of the war of October 1973 were attributed to the religious renaissance. But the peace concluded in 1978 is considered as a betrayal of the Arab-Muslim cause.

The halt of democratisation has made religious opposition the only answer to the control of civil liberties, exceptional laws and excessive recourse to referendums. While Nasser "persecuted" the Islamic organisations (from 1954 to 1966), placed al-Azhar under protection, supervised sermons in the mosques, and created a Ministry of Religion to provide guidelines for religious activity, Sadat deliberately drew support from these movements in order to reduce his enemies, extirpate Marxism, and use the fundamentalists to his advantage. Under his presidency the liberation of the Muslim Brothers, the construction of numerous mosques, the legislation on the sale and consumption of alcohol, the support of Muslim proselytism and showy religious practice, led to a climate favourable to Islamic activities and detrimental to the other currents of more secular and liberal thought.

The mass arrests of September 1981 were a sign of a late awakening to the immense danger implicit in this policy. After the assault of 6 October, Islamic activities have become more discreet. Although President Mubarak's slight dose of firmness and conciliation has created a certain detente, the causes of discontent still exist, and the Islamic revival remains a disturbing factor of national political life.

Islamic art

When the Arab tribes conquered Egypt, they engendered a renaissance of the art, literature and political institutions that had distinguished the country's illustrious past. Tent-dwelling nomads, whose only riches were their literature and their poetry, the Arab conquerors assimilated the artistic and architectural experience of the conquered land; consequently there was no abrupt break between Coptic and Islamic art. The latter borrowed many decorative motifs from the former, and the sultans did not hesitate to call upon Coptic architects to build their mosques.

Initially a simple covered building for prayers and meetings, the mosque rapidly became monumental. Beginning in the ninth century, a common plan was adopted for all the mosques in the Arab Empire. It provided for a rectangular open courtyard, the *sahn*, surrounded by several rows of arcades, often set off from the outside by a wall; between this wall and the mosque proper was the *ziada* with a fountain for ablutions. The direction of Mecca or *kibla* was indicated by a recess, the *mihrab*, which generally was profusely decorated. The pulpit or *minbar* was often made of carved or inlaid wood. Stucco, stone, or wood lace-work adorned the walls or described verses of the Koran. The dome, symbol of the vault of heaven, was introduced by the Fatimids; the minaret, which reaches toward the absolute, appeared around the seventh century. The architectural and ornamental forms evolved in the beginning under the influence of artists and planners gifted with remarkable technical skills inherited from earlier civilisations: Byzantine mosaic-work, for instance, or Coptic wood-carving. The common denominator was the Islamic faith, which prohibits the reproduction of the human figure and provides only the best for religious buildings.

The first mosque built by Amr at al-Fustat was made of sun-baked bricks and palm trunks, had no floor and was devoid of decoration. Rebuilt in the style of the great mosque of Damascus and brought up to its present size in 827, it was adorned with wooden friezes of acanthus-leaf motifs and stylised scroll-patterns of Coptic origin. It was repeatedly remodelled in later centuries, particularly in 1798, when the orientation of the aisles was changed and their number increased from six to twenty. The Nilometer at Roda dates from the same period. Built in 715, it was restored in the following century.

In building his mosque Ibn Tulun imitated the style of Samarra in Lower Mesopotamia. Built between 876 and 879, the Ibn Tulun mosque is made up of a large square courtyard ninety-two metres per side, framed on three sides by porticoes on columns, and including five aisles at the wall of the kibla; the broken arches are made of fired brick, a material imported from Mesopotamia. The sculptural decoration – in plaster, representing plant motifs with interlacing stems, a primitive form of the arabesque – makes up a marvellous frieze that runs around the top of the crenellation. The minaret, set outside the main building, has a spiral helix ramp whose mass diminishes from the bottom to the top. The wood carvings that the Tulunids have handed down to us are very impressive.

Under the Fatimids the Egyptian genius reached its full power of expression, thanks to the independence that the country enjoyed. A few memories of Tunisia, the first home of the dynasty, were kept alive in the mosque of al-Azhar. Begun in 970 and continually remodelled, fortunately with respect for the earlier constructions, the mosque is perhaps the most beautiful of Egypt. The al-Hakim mosque (990-1003), a porticoed construction, has preserved its original plan. The decoration of its projecting stone porches is remarkable; the minarets are also made of stone. The mosques of al-Akmar (1125) and al-Salih Talay (1160), with façades in cut stone, reflect a purer local tradition, successfully expressed again at al-Guyushi mosque (1085), the great dome of which was widely imitated. Its highly original minaret has three stories of diminishing dimensions, the first two square in plan, the third an octagon crowned by a small dome. The finest achievements of the Fatimids are unquestionably the fortifications of Cairo, which reflect the Byzantine tradition. The three monumental gates, Bab al-Nasr, Bab al-Futuh, and Bab Zuwela, are flanked by cubical or cylindrical towers that open on a central hall covered with soberly decorated vaults or domes.

The Ayyubite period has left only a few tombs and the citadel of Cairo, although it was at this time that the madrasas were created to re-establish orthodoxy. With an entrance designed to filter visitors, the madrasa was built to a cruciform plan with four monumental alcoves in the sahn for the four orthodox rites.

Under the Mamelukes the madrasa was fused with the mosque. Another innovation – the mausoleum of the founder – was added, at times composed of a tomb and chapel with raised domes decorated with geometric and floral lace-work. The model for this genre was the superb mosque of Sultan Hassan (1356-63). Between the mosque of Bibars (1266), the oldest, and that of al-Muayyad (1420), the most recent, that of Kalaun (1285) was built in a style of singular perfection. The mosque of Kait Bey (1472) is distinguished by its elegant and precious decoration, which includes a profusion of stalactites. Later additions to these mausoleums included the *sabil*, or water fountain, and the *kuttab*, a kind of primary school which underscores the persistent taste of the Egyptians for maintaining contact between the living and the dead.

After 1517 Egypt became a Turkish province. The Sultan Selim I took the best artists and architects with him to Istanbul, thrusting Egypt into a period of decadence. The mosque of Katkhuda (1734) maintained certain traditions, but the models prevailing at that time were the mosques of Brusa or Istanbul. During the eighteenth century these hybrid buildings combined the Mameluke style with the Ottoman, characterised by Byzantine vaults inspired by those of Hagia Sophia and slender, round minarets like those of the Turkish mosques. Ceramic tiles were replaced by revetments in faïence, like that of the Blue Mosque. The mosque of Mehmet Ali (1824-57), which dominates Cairo from the citadel, has been described as "a vision of the Bosphorus in the valley of the Nile."

As for the interior decoration of the mosques, in the ninth century stucco was used to make floral motifs in geometric frames and verses of the Koran around arches and windows. In the eleventh century open-work rosettes, niches and stalactites became increasingly common. In the fifteenth century the central courtyard, greatly reduced in size, was covered with a dome and illuminated by stained-glass windows. Wood carvings became increasingly abstract, but were embellished under the Fatimids with animals, stars and plants. The most beautiful wood carvings were reserved for pulpits and cenotaphs, of which two fine examples may be seen in the tombs of the saints Sayida Nefissa and Sayida Ruqiyya.

A new way of life

Eager for pomp and display, the kings who ruled Egypt after the Arab conquest developed a new way of life that brought all activities – political, military, artistic, commercial, intellectual and religious – under the patronage and control of the prince.

As early as the end of the Arab Conquest the Arab general Amr left Alexandria (which was too isolated from the rest of the valley and symbolised the Graeco-Roman occupation) to found a new capital at the gates of the fortress of Babylon at the point of the delta. Al-Fustat grew up amid vineyards and woodlands, soon extended northeast to al-Askar, was destroyed partially in 1168 under the crusades, then definitively under Bibars. In its place appeared a lake surrounded by orchards. Aesthetic concerns were never overlooked when planning towns. Al-Katai, the luxurious suburb created by Ibn Tulun, included princely residences as well as a race track, a menagerie of rare birds, sumptuous baths and a hospital. The multiple-storied brick buildings of al-Kahira, built by the Fatimids, were faced with cut stone, according to a contemporary traveller, and separated by orchards. The best secular art in Arabia is urban architecture, which was combined with the art of landscape gardening and with that of ornamen... ion. The town was the centre of economic life. The souks, or markets, were arranged according to their specialities – arms, jewellery, spices – around the mosque. The façades of houses presented alternating projections and alcoves that gave the streets a sinuous appearance; and their division into sections imparted a rhythm to the various neighbourhoods.

The fortified aristocratic quarter included the palaces and gardens of the caliph, his family and his dignitaries. It was the centre, in Muslim society, of material comfort, sensual pleasure and spiritual enlightenment – of oratorial contests, political debates, philosophical or doctrinal discussions, but also of feasts, music and dance, revelry and orgy.

The palaces were filled with precious objects that constituted the royal treasure: rugs and tapestries, sumptuous fabrics, brass or china ware, mosaic fountains. Finely carved or painted wood panels decorated the walls and framed the windows. The repertory of forms was even richer than that of religious monuments, where prohibitions limited the imagination. Figurative representations abounded: bronze reliefs, censors and wash basins in the form of real or imaginary animals with open-work carving; ceramic or wood friezes with dancing, hunting or banquet scenes; enamelled glass; rock-crystal water jugs; metalsmiths' work – all express a refinement that made these simple objects true works of art. Fabrics, ceramics and wood imitated the motifs in vogue in architecture, namely the linear forms of the Tulunid style, the trefoil motifs of Fatimid arabesques, or the geometric motifs and chinoiseries in fashion during the Mameluke period. The few extant rugs, with motifs borrowed from manuscript illuminations, calligraphy and Coptic art, are beautifully woven. Arms, armour and harnesses show the same concern for refinement. Cairo was unsurpassed for its stained-glass windows (a technique imported from Syria).

In accordance with the Islamic view of private life, and because of the heat of the climate, the traditional Egyptian house was turned inward. On the street, the windows were masked by shaped-wood *musharrabiya*; within, one or more gardens or courtyards lighted and cooled the surrounding rooms. The innermost part, reserved for the women, included a *hammam* (bath); the part for receiving guests was generally made up of a large room with a marble mosaic fountain, porches on the upper floor, and grilles of *musharrabiya* permitting women to watch ceremonies, concerts and dances without being seen. In the outbuildings were grouped the kitchen, bread-oven, wine-press and wells that provided the house with water. Until the close of the nineteenth century most domestic work was done by slaves, who were considered part of the family.

Having become the cultural, artistic and economic capital of Islam, Cairo, whose population was increasing, expanded beyond the town walls and yielded to the demands of urban development after the fall of the Fatimid dynasty.

106

105. The Sultan Hassan and El Rifai mosques in Cairo.

106-108. Islam is an essential component of the Egyptian national identity and is expressed in its language, art and architecture.

109. The mosque of al-Muayyad, built in 1420.

110. This small mosque near Beni Suef shows clearly the importance associated with the shape of the dome, symbolising heaven; here there is practically nothing else to the construction.

109

10

111. The sahn, or courtyard of the mosque of al-Hakim, built around the year 1000.

112

112. Ibn Tulun had this mosque built between 876 and 879 following the style of Samarra in Lower Mesopotamia. The columns of the arcade around the courtyard are made of fired brick, a material until then unknown in Egypt.

113. The Fatimid mosque of al-Hakim has preserved its original design.

114

115

114. Open-air café in El Minya, near Beni Hassan.

115. The freshly flayed skin of an animal in a street in Cairo. This is not an unusual sight; when a member of the family dies, for example, it is customary for the head of the family to kill an animal on the doorstep of the house and then to offer its meat to the poor.

116-117. Important religious ceremonies, like circumcisions and marriages, take place in a sort of marquee made of rugs or tapestries outside the house, in a courtyard or even in the street.

116

17

بسم الله الرحمن الرحيم
وبه نستعين
الطريقه الرفاعيه بيت
الله أكبر

118

119

118. View of the interior of a colonial-style café.

119-120. Khan el Khalili is a bazaar in Cairo where life takes place on the streets. Its stalls and shops sell everything, from antiques to objects in silver, copper or leather, as well as perfumes and spices.

121

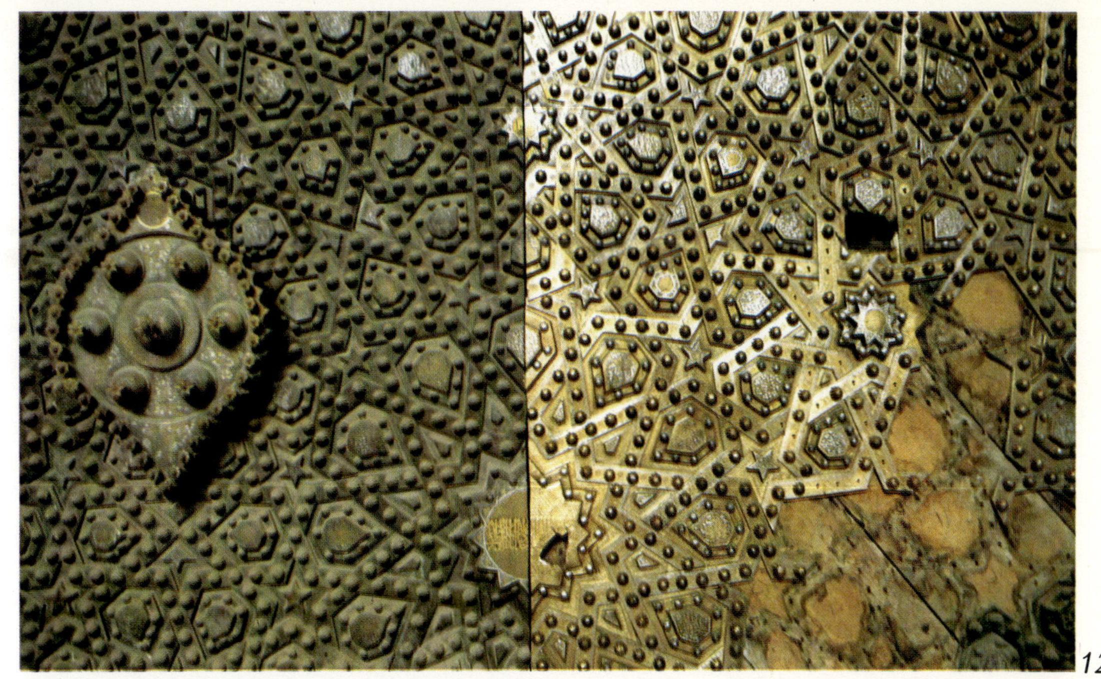

123

122

124

121-122. The Sultan Hassan mosque (1356-63) presents the innovations brought in by the Mamelukes; in particular the mausoleum of the founder, which acquires ever greater importance in the architecture of the mosque.

123. Detail of the elaborate decoration of one of the doors of the Sultan Hassan mosque.

124. Simple wall decorations, in non-precious materials, at times seem to emulate the great art forms of the past.

125

125-126. The Blue Mosque combines the Mameluke and Ottoman Styles, with Byzantine domes like those of Hagia Sophia in Istanbul and faïence ornamentations. In all mosques the direction of the Mecca is indicated by a recess, the mihrab, *elaborately decorated (126).*

127

127-128. The Mehmet Ali mosque in the Citadel in Cairo, built in the nineteenth century, has been described as "a vision of the Bosphorus in the valley of the Nile."

129-130. The al-Azhar mosque is today the seat of the Islamic university. It has always been not only the spiritual heart of Cairo, but also the political centre: at the time of important national events, it is here that the people gather. It was begun in 970 under the Fatimids and, although it was continually remodelled at later dates, it is perhaps the most beautiful mosque in Egypt.

128

29

131 

132 

131-132. Islamic faith prohibited the representation of the human figure, so that the artists and artisans who created the first mosques and their decoration made imaginative variations on floral and geometric motifs: the arabesque.

133. The interior of the Mehmet Ali mosque, in the Citadel.

134

135

136

137

134. The Abu al-Abbas mosque, in Alexandria.

135. View of the skyline of Alexandria from the port.

136. A street vendor selling liquorice juice. Alcoholic beverages are prohibited by the Islamic faith.

137. The handprint on the wall of this café in Alexandria is a common good luck symbol, believed to ward off the evil eye.

138

139

138-140. Religious festivities are the occasion for elaborate decorations with rugs and tapestries and also for displaying ex-votos in gratitude for the most varied occurrences.

الشيخ رفعت محمد القصاص
نائب السادة الرفاعية عن
محافظة البحيرة

141

142

14

144

141. A moment of prayer.

142. A bookshop in Cairo.

143. Wool carding in a street in Ataba.

144. A street near the Bab Zuwela gate in Cairo.

145

146

145. Heliopolis, now a suburb of Cairo, was a town built by the Belgians. This is the palace a Belgian baron built for himself: clearly a Belgian idea of what Egyptian architecture should look like.

146. Posters of President Sadat and President Mubarak during a national festivity.

147. View of the city of Cairo from the Citadel.

Modern Egypt

The awakening of Egypt

The awakening of Egypt began with the French expedition. When Napoleon landed at Abukir on 1 July 1798 in order to cut off British communications with the Indies, he found a country impoverished by brigandage, epidemics and administrative disorder. The defeat of the Mamelukes by the French completely discredited the former and prepared the way for their definitive removal. By giving the notables a hand in the civil administration and initiating a tax reform which proportioned contributions to the tax-payer's income rather than to the collector's appetites, the First Consul planted a seed of revolution that would grow later. But Nelson's destruction of the French fleet at Abukir forced the army to procure its provisions from the people; and the requisitions, tributes and other mandatory contributions that this entailed caused revolts that were bloodily repressed. The hostility of the populace contributed to the success of the British forces, which compelled the French to surrender on 2 September 1801. Despite its brevity and its scarse political consequences, the Napoleonic campaign opened a breach in the isolation of Egypt through which the country emerged into the vortex of international politics. The report that the team of experts who accompanied the French forces set down, and particularly the attention they drew to the possibility of building a canal between the Mediterranean and the Red Sea, contributed in no small measure to the broadening of European interest in Egypt.

Mehmet Ali, the creator of modern Egypt

Five years of disorders led by the young Turkish officer Mehmet Ali forced the English back to their boats and ousted the Mamelukes from power. Afterwards Mehmet Ali obtained a popular investiture and was proclaimed Pasha of Egypt, gaining the official recognition of the sultan on 9 July 1805. He endeavoured to build a modern State with the aid of European advisors, mainly from France. He replaced the Councils of the central administration with Ministries, and he regrouped the regional districts into seven Governorships, placing a Turkish governor at the head of each. Monopolising land, trade and industry, he conducted the country's affairs as if they were his own. This enabled him to plan agriculture in accordance with international trends. He leased land at exorbitant prices and used the revenue to finance colossal public works – such as the Mamudia Canal, which brought the Nile to Alexandria; a great dam at the point of the delta; a dense system of irrigation canals – all this without running the country into debt. He sold part of the crops stored at the burgeoning harbour of Alexandria to Europe through foreign mediators; and negotiated the remainder on a home market freed of competition by severe embargoes. Part of the considerable revenue generated by this monopoly and by those he established over cotton-spinning and sugar-refining was spent on building up a fleet and a 200,000-man army that won distinction in the campaigns of Ibrahim Pasha and assisted the Ottoman tutelage. In less than fifty years the Pasha of Egypt succeeded in making his country a Mediterranean power.

An ambitious educational system, organised with the cooperation of European educators and aided by foreign missions dispatched especially to France, favoured the creation of an intellectual elite. European economic and cultural influence increased as British and French advisors were called in to cover more and more leading governmental positions.

In foreign policy Mehmet Ali embraced the policy of his sovereign against the Wahhabids of Arabia, occupying Mecca and Medina. Encouraged by his success in these endeavours, he launched expansionistic campaigns, annexing first the Sudan, then Syria. He twice threatened Constantinople, in 1832 and 1839, quite nearly destroying the Ottoman Empire. But his ambition disturbed the great powers, who imposed their mediation following the destruction of the Turco-Egyptian fleet at Navarin. The London Convention of 1839 obliged Mehmet Ali to surrender his conquests, reduce his army to 18,000 men and suppress his fleet, but permitted him to retain, during his lifetime, his sovereignty over the Sudan. Through the mediation of France he obtained hereditary power in 1840. He died in 1849.

European imperialism

Whereas Mehmet Ali preferred to build dams rather than the "Canal of the two Seas" proposed by his advisors, his less prudent successors saw the opening of the Isthmus of Suez as a further means of diminishing the importance of the Porte. Begun by Saïd and inaugurated by Ismail in 1869, Ferdinand de Lesseps's canal completed the internationalisation of Egypt. Although the canal had a few felicitous consequences for the country (conspicuous increase of revenues; the creation of new towns; strategic importance, and diplomatic prestige), it placed Egypt at the mercy of her European creditors.

Saïd effected two social reforms that had important repercussions on the country's future. The first, promulgated in 1858, put an end to State capitalism and acknowledged the right to private property, giving rise to a landed middle class. The second opened the higher echelons of the army to Egyptians, creating a caste of nationalist officers which would play a vital role in the country's future.

To release Egypt from Turkish tutelage Ismail doubled the tribute due to the Porte. In exchange he obtained recognition of the right of succession in order of primogeniture for his descendents; the possibility to conclude international agreements; the right to increase the number of his troops; and the title of Khedive (1867). He initiated educational programmes, developed public works and created an Advisory Assembly, a State Council, and mixed courts which brought an end to the exorbitant privileges of the capitulary regime. In addition, he established a postal system, literary and scientific associations, and a museum of antiquities; and he extended the railway network. To cover the expense of this ambitious programme of modernisation as well as that of his military campaigns (expeditions in Crimea and in Mexico, conquest of the Sudan), the Khedive contracted high-interest loans. Driven to the verge of bankruptcy, he was forced to sell his shares in the Suez Canal to Great Britain at an exceedingly low price. The placement, in 1876, of his finances under audit by the European powers, who imposed an English Minister of Finance and a French Minister of Public Works, raised the contempt of the nation. Particular indignation arose among the younger army officers, whose salaries were no longer paid punctually, whose career advancement was blocked by their Turco-Circassian superiors, and who were expelled from the service in great numbers by the European control commission. To the cry of "Egypt to the Egyptians" a violent xenophobia developed that culminated in a rebellion of a group of officers led by Colonel Arabi Pasha. The latter imposed on Tawfig, the incoherent successor of Ismail (whom the sultan had destituted at the instigation of the British on 25 June 1879), several changes in home policy and a firmer attitude towards foreign demands. An intimidatory show of the French and English fleets off Alexandria was met with popular demonstrations in the town, which was shelled by the British after the rejection of their ultimatum. British forces landed in the port on 15 July and from Ismailia attacked the Egyptian troops from behind, defeating them at Tell el-Kebir in the delta on 13 September 1882.

While maintaining the legal appearance of independence, the British inaugurated an effective policy (directed by their Consul General and his advisors) of "ruling the ruling classes." To legitimise their presence, they presented themselves as defenders of both the interests of foreigners and minorities, and those of the European powers. They attempted to correct the chaotic situation into which the country had fallen, establishing a structured administration and repairing State finances while reducing taxes. They eliminated statute labour, built dams and improved the irrigation system in order to extend the arable land and make Egypt a vast cotton field for the mills of Manchester. A new army, trained and organised by British officers, was sent between 1896 and 1898 to reconquer the Sudan, which became a joint Anglo-Egyptian dominion in 1899.

But hostility to the occupying forces grew both in extent and in radicality. Two factors strongly contributed to the resurgence of a national consciousness: the rapid spread of printing and the promotion of a new class of landowners, whose numbers increased considerably following the progressive division of land.

Tawfig's successor, Abbas II, who tolerated the English domination with difficulty, drew nearer to the nationalist movement, which was led by the young French-educated lawyer, Mustapha Kamel. But Turkey's entrance into the First World War on the side of Germany in 1914 gave London the pretext for proclaiming a protectorate – temporarily, it maintained – over Egypt, and for deposing the Khedive as a means of assuring the security of the Suez Canal. Various wartime measures – martial law, censorship, increased military presence, price hikes – raised the level of tension and fired opposition to the protectorate. The nationalist movement came under the expert leadership of Saad Zaghlul, who proved his political acumen by opting for inaction during the war, but requesting the authorisation of the British to go at the head of a delegation or "Wafd" duly mandated by the Legislative Assembly to reclaim Egypt's right to independence at the Peace Conference, immediately after the armistice of 1918. The categorical denial of this request and the exile of Zaghlul to Malta transformed the anger of the Egyptian people into fury. Riots, sabotage, assassinations and strikes spread throughout the country, bringing about a complete paralysis. In the face of this outbreak London unilaterally granted Egypt independence with the Declaration of 28 February 1922. The document contained four singularly restrictive clauses that obliged Egypt to safeguard communications within the British Empire; provide for its own defense; and protect minorities, foreign interests, and the Sudan. Not readily accepted by public opinion, the Declaration was followed in 1923 by a Constitution establishing a parliamentary monarchy. The next thirty years witnessed a three-sided struggle between the Wafd, which enjoyed an indestructible popularity; the kings (first Fuad, then Faruk), who resented the constitutional limits imposed on their powers; and the occupation forces, who used the differences between the popular leaders and the sovereign to their own advantage. The consequent political instability culminated in the Anglo-Egyptian Treaty of 1936, which brought a formal end to the English occupation of the Canal Zone. After the abolition of the Capitulations at Montreux in 1837, Egypt was admitted to the League of Nations.

Its vital strategic position obliged Egypt to fulfil its pledge of military cooperation with Great Britain during the Second World War. Paradoxically, the English in 1942 compelled King Faruk, under the threat of deposition, to accept a Wafdist government presided by Zaghlul's successor Nahhas Pasha, who was their eager collaborator. This contribution to the Allied victory was rewarded with London's blessing of the creation of the League of Arab States in the Egyptian capital in 1945. But the Wafd, harassed by the large landowners, discredited by its collaboration with the British, and corrupted by power, no longer responded to the aspirations of Egyptian patriots, many of whom looked favourably on communism after the Russian victories. Organisations having fascist tendencies, such as the "Green Shirts," or puritanical religious organisms, as the "Muslim Brothers," engaged in terrorist activities that threatened public safety. The situation precipitated after the disastrous war in Palestine, the economic marasma, and the defective weapons scandal. King Faruk lost his last basis of support: the army. On 26 January 1952 Cairo was put to the torch by anonymous terrorists, and a grave incident at Ismailia degenerated into a rebellion that was subdued with difficulty. As the situation worsened, the military took action.

The "Egyptian" revolution

Whereas the "modernisation" of Egypt took place under foreign stimulus, its "Egyptianisation" was the work of the young army officers who seized power on 23 July 1952. After obtaining the king's abdication in favour of his son, they set up a civilian government under the control of the Revolutionary Council; the difficulties that ensued led them to dissolve the political parties and to take the reigns of government into their own hands. Their movement, though initially very popular, was ill-defined: it lacked a precise ideological basis. Highly considered by the United States for its moderation (embodied by the liberal and popular General Naguib), it enjoyed American support in its plea to London to evacuate the Suez Canal in 1954. The junta's first important act was the application of an agrarian reform that, though modest, shattered the power of the large landowners and brought the new regime the consensus of millions of fellahs eager for land. The Republic of Egypt was proclaimed on 18 June 1953 under the leadership of General Naguib; the position of prime minister was conferred on a young lieutenant colonel with a powerful and complex personality, Gamal Abdel Nasser. The rivalry between the two men ended in the elimination of the former. Nasser remained chief executive until his death, achieving an unprecedented breadth of popularity. His "Arab socialism" involved the State in all domains. It was sustained by a police regime which, although it did not spare the communists, was particularly active against the Muslim Brothers, who had attempted to overthrow the republic in 1954.

The radicalisation of Nasser's foreign policy was in part due to Western blunders: American pressures on Egypt to adhere to the Pact of Baghdad, the refusal to sell Egypt weapons, and the humiliating withdrawal of aid for the construction of the Aswan dam. These led Nasser to defy foreign imperialism and to reduce its hold on the country by nationalising the Suez Canal in July 1956. This sudden gesture resulted in a Franco-British military intervention and a second war with Israel as unfortunate as the first, but it also established Nasser as a charismatic leader throughout the Third World. After participating in the Afro-Asiatic Conference at Bandung in 1955, where he appeared as the antagonist of the great powers, he set forth the concept of "positive neutrality" and championed the cause of non-alignment, giving his country a role in world affairs it otherwise could not have played. At the height of his popularity after Suez, he was called upon to unify the Arab world; he created the United Arab Republic with Syria in 1958. As the standard-bearer of pan-Arabism, he achieved its greatest successes and suffered its bitterest defeats, namely the dissolution of the union with Syria in 1961, the swallowing-up of Yemen, and the tragic military error of June 1967. Weary of the incomprehension with which he was subsequently surrounded, he abandoned his former outlook in favour of the "Egypt first" policy of the Rogers Plan. His premature death at the age of fifty-two in September 1970 threw consternation even over his enemies and brought him a posthumous victory.

His First Vice-President Anwar Sadat inherited a very difficult situation. Breaking with the autocratic practices of his predecessor, Sadat proved skilful in eliminating his leftists opponents in May 1971. After restoring the name of Egypt, he granted amnesty to the Confraternity of Muslim Brothers and clamped down on the unions. On the morrow of the war of October 1973, he attempted an experiment in "pluralistic democracy." This did not have the expected success, however, and he toughened his regime, especially with regard to the communist left, and created the National Democratic Party, forcing his opponents off the political scene. But inflation, the growth of inequalities and the activities of the Muslim Brothers, whom Sadat had tolerated thus far, nourished a strong dissatisfaction that led the government to take action in September 1981 against its opponents on the left and right alike.

After obtaining massive armaments from the Soviet Union, Sadat expelled the Soviet military advisors in July 1972 and unleashed his great offensive against Israel on 6 October 1973. His military successes of the first days restored the pride of the Egyptian people and gave birth to an unprecedented Arab solidarity, the most spectacular manifestation of which was the total embargo on the oil exportations to the United States.

Once the Israeli debt had been paid, the Rais embarked on a spectacular new reconciliation with Washington. Since the solution of the Arab-Israeli problem was not making great progress, Sadat planned the historic visit to the Knesset in November 1977. This visit opened the way to direct negotiations, which led to the Agreements of Camp David in 1978, followed by the Washington Peace Treaty in March 1979. This caused a violent reaction among the Arab nations, and the interruption of diplomatic relations with Cairo by all but two – the Sudan and the Sultanate of Oman.

The intransigence of Israel, which forced Sadat to make numerous concessions, increased his isolation. He was assassinated by a group of Muslim integralists on 6 October 1981.

Economic and social change

Beginning in the nineteenth century the great works undertaken to hold back the flood waters of the Nile – earthen walls four to five meters wide; large, deep canals that make up actual branches of the river; great back-up dams along the entire length of the river from Cairo to Aswan – made it possible to irrigate a great part of the country throughout the year. The overlapping growing seasons assured three or sometimes even four harvests per year. The alluvium held back by the dams was replaced by chemical fertilisers, and to improve the soil and avoid its imbibition steps were taken to assure sufficient drainage as well as irrigation.

The advent of perennial irrigation profoundly altered the relation between the fellah and his land, which in turn led to radical economic and social changes. A veritable agricultural revolution followed the introduction of cotton and its extension over the land. Different varieties appeared in response to different soil types. The most famous of these, the long-fibre variety discovered by the French agronomist Louis Jumel, was subjected to a strict quality-control policy. In less than fifty years Egypt became one of the world's leading cotton producers and experienced unprecedented economic growth. By turning the entire life of the nation towards monoculture for export, and by precipitating the commercialisation of agriculture, the cultivation of cotton caused profound changes in the use of the land. The large landowners preferred a system of share-cropping or hired labour, which left a greater margin of profit than that of rents, the very low salaries of agricultural workers allowing substantial gains. Consequently, the small farmers were gradually forced off the land and transformed into agricultural labourers.

The population explosion

To keep salaries low the latifundists encouraged a high birth rate. Assisted by prosperity, Egypt witnessed a prodigious population increase. Estimated at 2.5 million in 1800, the population had risen to 6,800,000 by the time of the first official census in 1882. According to a report published on 14 October 1982 by the central statistical office in Cairo, the nation now has 45,000,000 inhabitants and an annual growth rate of 1,200,000 persons, or an Egyptian every 27 seconds. At this dizzying pace (an annual increase of 34 per 1000, one of the highest in the world) Egypt is rapidly becoming overpopulated. Arable land is relatively scarse (36,000 square km), and the population density today exceeds 1000 inhabitants per square km. The absence of emigration, a longer average life expectancy, and a decrease in infant mortality of around 60% during the first fifty years of the century have further increased the demographic pressure. Between 1897 and 1960, while the population increased by 370%, the arable land increased by 20%. Egyptian agriculture is already well developed and its output is quite high (the production of cotton is unsurpassed in the world and the yield of corn is equal to that of the United States).

One of the most obvious solutions to this explosive problem is, and always has been, to reclaim new land from the desert, which implies control of the flood waters. The latest achievement in this connection is the dam at Aswan, the realisation of which followed tumultuous political events and the nationalisation of the Suez Canal in 1956. Begun in January 1960 and inaugurated in January 1971, today it holds the river behind an imposing mass 3600 metres long, 980 metres wide at the base and 40 metres at the summit, forming the world's largest man-made lake, Lake Nasser, 500 km long and 10 km wide. Thanks to this dam, year-round irrigation is assured to Upper Egypt, and it is hoped that the new areas reclaimed from the desert will increase the arable land by one third.

The agrarian reform

The junta of "Free Officers" that came into power in July 1952 had three basic policy goals: to correct the poor distribution of land through the application of an agrarian reform that would do away with the more glaring inequalities and orient private capital towards industry; to improve the land in such a way as to produce the greatest benefit for the greatest number; and actively to promote industrialisation.

The agrarian reform, applied from the outset, was accompanied by a number of other measures designed to establish more efficient relations in the rural world. These included the imposed lowering of rents, fixed at seven times the amount of the land tax; the abolition of agrarian debts; the creation of cooperatives for the distribution of fertiliser, seeds, and credit; the diversification of crops; and the protection of livestock. To combat the subdivision of farm plots a policy was enacted in 1960 which provided for the reorganisation of parcels of land, according to the nature of the crops grown, into larger use-units subject to double or triple rotation, the sale of whose products was guaranteed by the State.

The most spectacular result of the agrarian reform was that it brought an end to the shocking inequality in the distribution of land, eliminating the class of large landowners, trading intermediaries, and parasites of all kinds, including village usurers. Although it shifted the centre of gravity of the agrarian structure and introduced more productive relations in the rural world, it also extended the competency of the cooperatives over numerous domains, leading to a proliferation of bureaucracy and all that it entails: inefficiency, higher costs, waste and corruption; and discouraged private initiative. Moreover, the State's efforts to transfer surplus capital from agriculture to other fields often led simply to reduced yields.

It is undoubtedly early to weigh the positive and negative aspects of the Aswan dam. The complementary projects designed to implement its potential benefits – particularly the great drainage works – have not yet been carried out, for want of funds. By bringing the river under control it has certainly served a regulatory purpose. Thanks to the constant availability of water, it is now possible to irrigate the entire country, even in summer. Its negative aspects are unfortunately all too evident. They include holding back the fertile alluvium, which must be substituted by costly and anti-ecological chemical fertilisers; erosion of the river bed, its banks and canals, and the Mediterranean coast; and elevated salinity of the soil due to the relatively stable water level – just to mention the most obvious.

The reclamation of desert land has not proceeded at the expected pace, as it requires considerable expenditures that are not always justified by the scarse yields of the first years.

Industrialisation

Mehmet Ali's industrialisation efforts – consisting in the development of cotton mills and sugar refineries – had no following. His successors brought no significant improvement and the British occupation forces, which controlled the country after 1882, systematically opposed innovation. But because of the destruction they caused elsewhere, the two world wars favoured the development of local industry. Following the First World War the cotton boom and the economic well-being that accompanied it brought new wealth to the country, permitting the establishment in 1920 of the first bank with Egyptian capital and of numerous collateral firms. The Second World War provided an even greater stimulus to industrialisation. On the eve of the 1952 Revolution the industrial sector represented 15% of the gross national product, employed about 8% of the work force, and brought in 9.6% of the profits in foreign currency by exportation.

The regime established in 1952 promoted extensive State participation in national life. Its investment policy gave high priority to the development of heavy and medium industries – iron and steel mills, fertiliser plants and electric power stations. Egyptianisation of the civil administration; nationalisation and utilisation of confiscated land; industrial investment and production; administration (from 1956 on) of the Suez Canal and of expropriated Anglo-French property – all these factors contributed to the creation of a bureaucracy that grew year after year (thanks also to the obligation of each organism to hire a certain annual quota of university graduates even if there was no work for them to do) until it reached the point of paralysis. The hold of the public sector on the economy enabled the regime to satisfy its clientele, to control the means of financing its programmes and to eliminate all opposition that might interfere with its plans of development; but it weighed heavily on business as a whole.

After the war of 1973 President Sadat placed economic development at the head of his priorities. He broke all ties with the Nasser administration, inaugurating his policy of *infitah*, or opening towards the West. This policy was based on a reorganisation of the banking system and on laws favouring foreign investments. To instill confidence, Sadat returned the property confiscated by his predecessor, and he increased the number of major projects. These came to include the development of the Suez Canal Zone; the construction of towns and harbours and a 10,000 Megawatt hydroelectric plant in the Kattara depression in the Libyan desert; the development of the New Valley in the south; the creation of factories; the development of the production of fertiliser, cement and agricultural products; and the stimulation of oil prospecting. To decongest the Nile valley, desert areas were to be parcelled out and new towns to be built. After 1978, in anticipation of a possible Arab boycott, Egypt sought increased Western support. In 1981 the United States, France, West Germany, Japan, Great Britain and Italy were its principal partners. Reimbursement of borrowed funds was guaranteed by the return of around sixty billion francs from five essential sources: petroleum and gas, which after the recent discoveries and the restitution of the Sinai wells represented 35 million metric tons of hydrocarbons annually; the transfers effected by more than four million Egyptian expatriates; the Suez Canal; tourism; and cotton.

This open policy had serious drawbacks. Applied immediately after a costly war and under difficult economic conditions, it broadened the cleavage between rich and poor and increased real-estate speculation in the larger cities. Certain favourites who acted as intermediaries between foreign businessmen and the omnipresent public sector rapidly accumulated fortunes. Their lifestyle differed greatly from that of the majority of the population, which was compelled to buy food at subsidised prices and use inefficient public transportation that was increasingly costly with respect to the parsimonious wages. Furthermore, the defence budget, the financing of development programmes, the massive importation of basic goods at a value of more than twenty billion francs annually contributed to the accumulation of an enormous foreign debt that was made worse by inflation (around 25%) and the plethoric development of tertiary activities (four million civil servants).

Much hard work awaits President Mubarak. He will have to arrest the course of inflation, distribute the social burdens more equitably, popularise birth control, suppress the intermediaries and restore life to the sectors paralysed by bureaucracy.

Daily life in the countryside

The traditional peasant culture of Egypt has remained essentially unchanged. Today nearly half the population is employed in agriculture and lives in the country, in some 4,224 villages and 24,000 hamlets. Although it is the basis of a hierarchical society, the peasantry has always been relegated to a position of inferiority. Little understood by city dwellers, it is a separate world with its own rites and beliefs.

Although the conservatism of the peasantry is a universal phenomenon, that of the Egyptian peasantry surpasses all others. Many writers have pointed out the immutability of the rural landscape and of the fellahs' way of life. In many cases peasants continue to use the same tools that were used in ancient Egypt – the hoe (*fas* in Arabic), that all-purpose implement for tilling the soil, weeding and keeping up canals, is identical today to that represented in the tombs of the pharaohs. Archimedes's screw, the *shaduf* – a movable pole mounted on a base, with a pail attached to a rope at one end and a large stone at the other – an ancient means for drawing water, is still to be found throughout the land. The scythe and wheel-plough were for a long time snubbed in favour of the primitive swing-plough.

The age-old annual cycle of flood, seedtime and harvest was respected up till the nineteenth century. At flood time the water spread out to form immense pools from which the villages, built on higher land, emerged as islands surrounded by palm-trees. Communication between villages was effected by boat. The fellah devoted this idle period to his favourite pastimes – such as fishing – or to handicrafts. Today irrigation and drainage canals criss-cross the countryside, bringing life-giving water to all usable land. The chequered fields stretch away out of sight, dominated here and there by palm-trees, sycamores and weeping willows. From one year to the next up to three crops may be harvested, their colours changing from pale green to golden yellow. The soil never rests, and the fellah, who goes into the fields at dawn and returns at dusk, is rarely able to relax. The pattern of settlement – in densely populated villages – minimizes the encroachment of homesteads on productive farmland, protects the population from intrusion, provides for solidarity among the farmers, and makes possible the use of community tools. The villages fit naturally into the landscape, sometimes surmounted by the minaret of the mosque, the dome of a saint, or one of the dovecotes in which the peasant architectural imagination is concentrated; for the houses, huddled around the tortuous streets, are all alike. Built by their inhabitants, they are generally made of sun-baked brick covered with mud. At the centre is a courtyard and stable from which access is gained to two or three rooms, one of which contains an oven; here the family sleeps in winter to keep warm. The flat roof is used in summer to take the cool night air, and at other times to store firewood, corn stalks, cotton-plants, compost and earthenware vessels containing grain and oil. Household furnishings are spare and primitive. Windows are few and small, except in the houses of notables, which are generally made of fired brick or stone. The Nile or a canal of greater or lesser importance is always to be found nearby and forms the centre of village life. Here ducks and geese splash about, and the women wash their clothes or their crockery. When their work is done, they fill their *ballas* (jugs) and majestically carry them on their heads to their homes, where they will pour the contents through a *zir*, or rudimentary earthen filter. Throughout the countryside men till the fields; donkeys trot merrily along the canals, pulling carts loaded with alfalfa or manure; and dromedaries, barely visible beneath trusses of sugar cane or corn, lope along at their heavy, rhythmic pace, accompanied by the resounding groan of the *sakiehs* (norias), whose wheels of buckets turned by blindfolded waterbuffalo unceasingly draw irrigation water from the canal.

The standards of living of wage-labourers, farmers and small landholders do not differ much. Their diet is qualitatively and quantitatively insufficient. Vegetarians by necessity, they live chiefly on onions, green beans, pimentoes and cucumbers, with a bit of fermented cheese (the famous *mesh*) and cornmeal cakes. The evening meal is the most substantial: vegetables cooked in melted butter with rice and tomatoes. Meat is eaten on special occasions only.

The agrarian reform of 1952 brought an end to the glaring inequalities in the distribution of land, eliminating the old stratum of large landowners, cotton merchants, brokers, intermediaries and local money-lenders (who frequently profited by the farmers' tendency to prefer mortgage capital to working capital). In so doing the reform created a new class of wealthy peasants that replaced the former landed aristocracy, acquiring political and economic importance in the rural world. But it did not and could not solve the agrarian problem altogether, so great was the imbalance between population growth and the extension of arable land. This imbalance expressed itself in terms of unemployment and the consequent migration of the population from the country to the urban centres, the attraction of which was stronger where there were greater possibilities of employment. To escape from this sterilising state of alienation, the fellahs, who had previously been ineradicably loyal to their villages, began after some ten or twenty years to emigrate to other countries, chiefly within the Arab world. Today, for instance, there are more than two million Egyptian farmers in Iraq. The money they send is reinvested in their native villages, which little by little come forth from their isolation and are "modernised." Thanks to modern means of transportation (buses and collective taxis), fellahs may now reach the larger regional centres with ease, and they may transport their goods from the country to the cities, which today have their own market structures, universities and services – all things that were previously unknown. There they sell their produce and buy the fruits of technology: butane stoves, radios, televisions and refrigerators.

Hospitality and solidarity

Despite the backbreaking labour that working the land requires, the fellahs love life intensely. In this respect they resemble their distant ancestors – who did all they could to perpetuate life after death – and subscribe fully to their adage: "Follow your heart and the pleasures you desire. Do as you like on earth, but do not confine your heart. The day will come in which you, too, will be lamented, but the cries will not deliver a man from the other world. Enjoy the moment, without fatigue. Alas, no one can take his riches with him; what is gone cannot be regained." Almost all salutations in Egypt are wishes of longevity: "Let Allah give you long life," "That you should live and be happy," "Allah keep you alive." To someone who has lost a friend or relation, one would say in consolation "that the days he did not live should be added to yours"; the response, "that your life should continue."

The fellahs turn the various moments of their lives into songs in which they express joy or suffering, hatred or desire. They sing while they work, or afterwards, in the evening, with day-labourers, camel- and donkey-drivers; and their songs are almost always improvised. In hard work requiring more than two hands, a whole chorus sings out in cadence the effort needed; boatmen pole or row their boats ahead to the rhythm of their chants. Each province has its own songs. Each village has its own poet, wedding dancers and professional musicians who play the guzia or the tambourine – and for solemn events, its own religious singers who chant verses of the Koran.

Because of their natural propension toward good humour, the fellahs easily enjoy themselves. They adore jokes, word-plays and puns. In spite of the attachment they feel to the land, centuries of extortion and tyranny have made them distrustful, and they harbour the conviction that the oppressor can be got the better of in good conscience. To apply this principle to all authority, especially that of the State, considered by its very nature tyrannical and rapacious, requires a very small step indeed, which they happily take.

Although not aggressive by temperament, the fellahs are nevertheless quick-tempered and quite touchy in questions of honour. In certain regions – and particularly in Upper Egypt where the population is more violent – family antagonisms often degenerate into village feuds in which deaths are not uncommon. The police is always at a loss to discover the guilty parties, who vanish into the fields of sugar cane. Because these affairs must be settled personally, each man making it a point of honour to do justice himself, the victim is not mourned until his people have avenged his death. The quarrels sometimes originate with the misconduct of a daughter, seduced by a young member of another clan. The males of the family – father, brothers and cousins – are then obliged to cleanse the family honour in blood, by killing the guilty party and his accomplice.

Its hospitality and solidarity are the greatest virtues of the rural world. As deprived as he may be, a fellah will share what he has with those who are less fortunate. Hospitality is sacred, and he will bring out all his provisions in honour of his guest, without a second thought. In provincial towns, where there are often no hotels, the notables keep their house and their table open to travellers and expect nothing in return. Mutual aid is practised on a large scale: if someone is hindered from working by accident or illness, his work is done by his friends or neighbours. Widows and orphans are never forgotten on holidays.

The fellahs are generally very religious. They pray five times a day at home and on Friday at the mosque; and they rarely neglect to visit the tombs of the saints. This does not prevent them from being superstitious. They strongly believe in the evil eye, cast by envy, the dreaded attacks of which require an entire arsenal of formulas to thwart their effects – amulets hung around the necks of children, who are the most vulnerable; but also blue beads hitched to the halters of animals, or rams' horns hung above the entrance to the home. If the evil manages to get through despite all precautions, one may fight it off by throwing alum or salt into the fire or burning incense throughout the house. Everyone believes in the effectiveness of written curses and charms. One fear particularly afflicts the fellahs: the *afarit*, pre-adamite beings whose element is fire, who live underground but can come to the surface and penetrate the body of certain persons, whom they ceaselessly torment. These persons have no choice but to consult a magician, whose book contains incantations, orders and charms that enable him to establish the protective talisman. In more serious or difficult cases, curious magic rites of exorcism called *zar* are organised; these can last several days and involve animal sacrifices and ritual dances.

Important ceremonies

Their taste for festivities is such that the fellahs do not hesitate to upset the precarious equilibrium of their family budget, or even to exceed it with debts, in order to celebrate in a suitable manner.

Their love of children means that every birth – and especially that of a boy – is welcomed with joy. The life of the male child is marked by two important ceremonies, his circumcision and his marriage. The former generally takes place around the age of eight, the celebrant being the village barber. Wearing a cap with tassels and a cashmere shawl, the youth parades through the village streets on a richly caparisoned horse, preceded by musicians. The next day the barber takes the boy, now dressed in a long-sleeved white robe, and cuts his foreskin, which he roles in one of his sleeves where it remains until the healing of the wound, washed every day with henna. On the seventh day the skin is placed in a date, which is set in a loaf of bread. This is thrown into the Nile as an offering, as one recites the ritual formula, "take this, our last offering; return it to us as joy, peace, and strength."

When he reaches the age of eighteen – the minimum required age – or after his mandatory military service, the young man's parents think of getting him married, preferably to his maternal cousin or another village girl who has celebrated her sixteenth spring. During a first ceremony called *katb el Ketab* (signing of the contract), he goes to the home of his future father-in-law accompanied by two witnesses. He delivers the *mahr* (marriage settlement) agreed upon; and, before the *maazun* (civil servant), he shakes the hand of the bride's father under the ritual handkerchief. The latter, as his daughter's *wakil* (proxy), pronounces the phrase that seals the marriage: "I give you my daughter for your wife"; the groom answers: "I accept her as my bride. I promise to take care of her and protect her. Those who are present here, bear witness." After the contract has been signed the girl's father offers his guests dinner.

On the eve of the wedding the young woman's mother and future mother-in-law depilate and wash her body, and smear the palms of her hands and the soles of her feet with a henna paste held in place with small ribbons; her friends call on her and press coins, their wedding presents, into the henna paste. This is the so-called henna evening. The next day, all the bride's furniture – bed, mattress, chest, sofa and crockery – placed in plain view on a cart (in the past, the vehicle was a camel) is brought to her future home, preceded by musicians. The following day is that of the *dokhla* (consummation). The bride, wearing a beautiful gown and all her jewellery, her eyes lined with *kohl*, enters the groom's home before sunset. Meanwhile her friends execute belly-dances and sing around her while awaiting supper. The men are served first, on low tables. The menu includes chopped meat served with ground wheat, stews and stuffed vegetables, followed by pastries, candied fruit and puddings. After the meal they retire beneath a tent gaily decorated with paper lanterns and flags to drink coffee and smoke; the groom's friends, who offered him the day before a lamb, sugar, coffee and rice, execute a "stick dance," simulating combat, in his honour, as guns are fired outside as a sign of festivity.

An ancient tragedy

Influenced by their belief in predestination, the Egyptians display exemplary patience before the vicissitudes of life, and resignation and remarkable courage in the face of death. These qualities, however, do not preclude shows of despair whose excesses are unequalled elsewhere. The women of the family in mourning go about the village dressed in black, spreading the news with piercing cries. They are accompanied by professional mourners waving black, blue or green handkerchiefs. They precede the procession, enveloped in blue veils (blue is the colour of mourning, as in ancient Egypt), their heads, arms and chests covered with dust. At the moment of consigning the body the tumult reaches its peak; and an animal, whose meat will be distributed among the needy, is killed on the doorstep of the house. The sacrifice is supposed to help the soul of the deceased to leave his home and to present himself before his Judge; as well as to ward off new misfortunes. It may sometimes be made over the grave. In the funeral procession the friends of the deceased take turns carrying the litter, chanting the Islamic profession of faith. After a prayer at the mosque, the men proceed to the cemetery, where the body is buried amidst the earth, the face turned toward Mecca. During the first night the deceased will have to answer for his actions in this life as two angels, *Munkar* and *Madir*, come to question him. His fate in the next world depends on the outcome of this interrogation. Increasing numbers of villagers bring their condolences to the unfortunate house, where everyone does his share to provide refreshments for the visitors.

Concern for the dead is an essential part of the Egyptians' existence. To assure the deceased's happiness in the next world, relations make periodic visits to the grave, bearing offerings (dates, dry cakes, round loaves of bread) to distribute in their name among the readers of the Koran, the mourners at other graves and the poor. Before leaving their loved ones, they place palm fronds over the grave and sprinkle it with water, to quench the thirst of the deceased.

The similarities between these rites and the ceremonies of ancient Egypt are striking. Then as now one went in procession to the cemetery to bring offerings to the dead. The incense burned over the grave, the animals that are sacrificed, the palm fronds laid down, the wailing and the maculations with indigo and dirt perpetuate very old rites that neither Christianity nor Islam have been able to suppress.

Cairo: a megalopolis of twelve million inhabitants

Cairo is the leading city of Africa and one of the more important cities in the world. Today it counts more than twelve million inhabitants – about a quarter of the country's population – in an area 35 km long and 15 km wide. This colossus, the concrete image of Egypt's political and social problems, is relatively young. From a medieval town with a reasonably slow growth rate, in less than a hundred years the Egyptian capital has become a giant megalopolis that poses unsurmountable difficulties for town planners and administrators. To explain this phenomenon one must go back several decades in time. Curiously, Mehmet Ali, so enterprising in other matters, showed little interest in his capital (he no doubt feared the uprisings of its population), reserving his predilection for Alexandria, which had rapidly become a centre of international trade. Credit for the modernisation of Cairo goes to the Khedive Ismail. Impressed by the accomplishments of Baron Haussmann during a journey to France in 1867, he decided to make his capital, on the eve of the opening of the Suez Canal, a city organised in the European manner. A network of avenues linking together a dozen squares was opened northwest of the old town, forming a new quarter that included an English garden (the Ezbekieh) and an opera house. Ismail contracted European firms to bring water to the new quarter and to light the streets with gas. This juxtaposition of an old center and a new "European" district prefigured the "colonial" city type, which brings together two utterly different worlds. The foreign occupation accentuated this quality.

The tumultuous Suez affair of 1956, which gave Egypt back to the Egyptians, completely changed the face of the capital. Today the old town, the decline of which started at the beginning of the century, continues to play an important role. It receives a substantial part of the rural exodus, estimated at 100,000 new arrivals per year, giving rise to a population density in the order of 26,000 inhabitants per square km, reaching peaks of 140,000 in certain popular neighbourhoods. All available housing exhausted, the homeless have even occupied Cairo's ancient cemeteries. Despite the proliferation of emergency shelters (such as tents on rooftops), and the construction of high-rise apartment buildings, the old town retains many signs of the past in its remarkable architectural complexes, which bear witness to the capital's splendid history. Although the traffic and noise of major thoroughfares alter the charm of certain areas, other small islands – fortunately preserved – retain a medieval peacefulness, their crooked winding streets lined with shops specialising in spices, gold or copper. The prestigious covered bazaar of Khan el Khalili, where no automobile traffic is allowed to enter, is still the delight of tourists, with its shops selling antique woodwork, pharaonic, Coptic, Muslim or Turkish antiquities, silver, copper and leather products, or precious essences.

The poor housing conditions that prevail in the popular quarters compel the inhabitants of these areas to live in the street, which consequently bustles with activity. The shops of craftsmen, knife-grinders, tailors, basket-makers, mattress-carders, weavers and barbers – which usually open directly onto the street – conceal little of their daily work. Pedlars find their last refuge in these highly animated streets. Carrying their merchandise on their heads or pushing it on two-wheeled hand-carts, they offer fish or vegetables, poultry in palm-leaf cages, cheese or fruit, calling their ware to the customer with a cry whose particular modulation signals their specialty. Mobile kitchens on carts with windows, serving food in the street, are quite common in these neighbourhoods. The menu is frugal: *koshari*, a mixture of rice, lentils and noodles in a spicy tomato sauce; fried potatoes and aubergines; chick peas or fish with salad; or, in the best of cases, omelettes stuffed with mashed beans. The western part of the city, which monopolises administrative and service activities while also comprising the residential areas that span the Nile, is less developed. At rush hour the traffic nears paralysis and pours into El Tahrir square (the great centre on which all roads converge), around which elevated walkways have been installed for pedestrian safety. The modern buildings of the business district, which have replaced the villas and gardens of the past, are falling to pieces for want of maintenance. In the better neighbourhoods, wherever space permits, high-rises of thirty floors and more spring up, especially along the Nile, which flows for many kilometres between a double wall of buildings that now conceals the minarets and domes of the mosques that used to dominate the skyline.

Today Cairo is a fascinating and disquieting city of brutal contrasts, in which ancient and modern monuments, poor and wealthy neighbourhoods stand side by side. This juxtaposition of two parallel and totally disproportionate economic levels is potentially dangerous, despite an apparent social cohesion resulting, in part, from the survival of a certain spirit of village solidarity. The social imbalances partially explain the recent emergence of groups of Muslim fundamentalists who exploit the difficult situation in order to question the country's relations with the outside world and who reject the values that have not brought the well-being that was expected.

The daily existence of such a mass of human beings is a source of innumerable difficulties. The public services are unable to cope with the work required of them. The water and electricity supplies are subject to interruptions that exasperate the populace. The sewage system and pumping stations are so overloaded that they periodically threaten to explode. The collectors overflow, particularly in the popular neighbourhoods, and the municipality does its best to fill the gaps. The collection of refuse is afflicted by want of finances, and the telephone network works in a haphazard way. One of the most difficult problems is posed by traffic, because of the size of the capital and the sheer magnitude of daily movement: more than 4,500,000 people use public transportation daily. Buses, extremely insufficient in number, soon fall to pieces beneath the weight of the masses that crowd them every day. The lifting of restrictions on the importation of private cars has caused more congestion; and hundreds of thousands of hand- or animal-drawn vehicles, together with a lack of respect of the most elementary rules of driving and parking, further aggravate the problem. Elevated expressways that pass over streets and squares have alleviated traffic somewhat, though not nearly enough.

Numerous plans have been put forth to solve these problems. The chief solution thus far has been to create satellite towns on the outskirts of the city without encroaching on precious farmland. The first of these towns, Madinet Nasr between Cairo and Heliopolis, ended up as a half-failure. Five others are planned, and one or two have been begun; but exorbitant costs and the difficulty of attracting employment-producing investments allows for only moderate optimism.

The Egyptians

The physical type of the Egyptians of the valley resembles that which one sees carved in pharaonic bas-reliefs: the peasants have the same thin, muscular body (with a tendency towards plumpness in the notables or bureaucrats); the same black, curly hair and dark, almond eyes (with a few blue-eyed blondes, vestiges of the invasions); and the same copper-coloured skin and straight profile with high cheek-bones, full lips and large nose.

At the edge of the desert are the tent-camps of Bedouin tribes, some of which are sedentary, while others remain nomadic. The Bedouins chiefly raise livestock – sheep or camels – and may be clearly distinguished from the fellahs by their features and clothing. Their women show only their eyes, concealing their faces behind black veils embroidered with sequins. The Bedouins are distrusted by the peaceful and stationary population of the valley, who consider them thieves. In the south, on the Sudanese border, live the dark-skinned, fine-featured Nubians. They have preserved their language and customs. The poverty of their region compells them to descend the Nile to seek employment in the major cities. Particularly appreciated for the excellence of their services and their integrity, they commonly find positions in hotels and middle-class households. Today they prefer to settle in the Aswan region, industrialised after the construction of the dam, which in many cases has flooded their gaily decorated villages along the river, forcing them to emigrate towards the north.

The Egyptians are generally quite witty. They are famous for their jokes, amusing stories called *nokat* that they tell about themselves and their faults. These become ferocious when directed toward the person or decisions of their leaders, as expressions of opposition.

Indolent by nature – the fellahs excluded – Egyptian men love to brouse slowly through the streets, to sit around the terraces of cafés and watch the passersby, play backgammon, or take a siesta. They like to enjoy life, because time for them is not money. The passage of a pretty girl in the street may provoke exclamations of admiration but never anything less proper (departures from accepted behaviour are severely repressed); for paradoxically the customary moderation and frugality of Egyptian men vies with a forceful sensuality enhanced by the climate, the practice of polygamy, and the ease of obtaining a divorce.

Herodotus called the Egyptians "the most religious of all men." Here in fact arose the idea of God and of immortality. Their pride in belonging to the community of "true believers" creates in Egyptian Muslims a certain superiority towards those who do not share their faith. They fulfil their religious obligations with punctuality, and on Friday the prayer rugs overflow into the streets around the mosques, without regard for the traffic. The Egyptians invoke God continually, to solicit His protection, thank Him for His mercy, or ask that He witness their good faith. Visits to the burial-places of the saints (who are invoked to solve their problems), and to those of deceased relations, are sacred obligations.

In a country where segregation of the sexes is still generally the rule, and where television, with programmes of questionable quality, is the only collective means of amusement, great celebrations that interrupt the routine of day-to-day life take on enormous importance, enabling the Egyptians to satisfy their inclination for uproarious entertainment.

The first ten days of the Muslim lunar year, in the month of Moharram, have a special *baraka* that makes every charitable deed even more worthy. Crowds flock to the al-Husseini mosque where *zikrs* (commemorations) are chanted without interruption in increasingly rapid rhythmic rounds punctuated by calls of "ya Allah." The departure of pilgrims for Mecca, the most important act in the life of the faithful, is marked by elaborate official ceremonies, accompanied by cannon-fire and processions that begin at the mosque of al-Azhar. The pilgrims' return is no less important: to welcome them their neighbours prepare their houses with special care, decorating the façades, in the villages, with naive drawings. Relations and friends come to congratulate the happy *hajj* and to benefit by a little of the holy *baraka* that they bear with them. They generally receive a gift from the holy land – water from the holy well (*Zam Zam*), a piece of the *kiswa* of the Kaaba, which is substituted each year, a bit of dust from the tomb of the Prophet, incense, palm fibres, and other products of the two holy cities of Hedjaz. The seventh day after their return ends with a *zikr*.

Of all the commemorations of saints, that of the birth of the Prophet, *Muled el-Nabi*, is considered the most important. It is prepared eight days in advance, during which time ceremonies and festivities abound. Activity is concentrated in al-Husseini square, near the al-Azhar mosque. Paper lanterns and flags decorate the tents set up for the occasion. Sugar dolls dressed in brightly-coloured paper clothes, sugar-cakes with sesame seeds or chick peas, *lukum*, and nougats are sold on tray baskets in the middle of the street. Singers and satirists entertain the crowd all through the night; and religious processions and *zikr* follow one another until the muezzin's call to morning prayer. The month of Ramadan, the ninth month of the year, is devoted to fasting. Activity slows down and a general torpor sets in. A little before sundown, everyone rushes home to break the fast as soon as the muezzin's call resounds. The meal, always more elaborate and abundant than a usual meal, is accompanied by precious almonds, walnuts, hazelnuts and dried figs, which strict currency regulations allow to be imported only during the holy month. In the evening all the mosques are lighted and the minarets ringed with lanterns. The shops remain open until dawn. After the meal, one goes visiting or promenades through the streets, where the liveliness grows as the night progresses. Cinemas, theatres and cabarets are extraordinarily full. Peaceful citizens, transformed into night-rovers, are sullen the day after. The Koran was sent to the Prophet on the night of the twenty-seventh day of Ramadan. Notwithstanding its solemnity, this month is lived in gaiety, equality and fraternity. It concludes with three days of great rejoicing during which one goes to numerous banquets, filling up on sweets and dainties. The dead are not forgotten; during this time one visits their graves, bearing offerings that draw them into the general merriment.

The Feast of the Sacrifice, also called the Great Feast, which takes place on the tenth day of the last month of the year, *Zul Haggah*, is celebrated in much the same way, though with perhaps a bit less uproar. On this day a lamb is sacrificed in commemoration of the trial of Abraham.

The great popular feasts that marked the various phases of the Nile have all disappeared, except that of spring, *Sham en-Nessim* (Inspiration of the Zephyr), which is still celebrated on the Coptic Easter Monday by virtually all the populace without regard to age, sex or religion. The theme of the holiday is the rebirth of plant life. Beginning at dawn crowds flock to the green areas of the city – the residential neighbourhoods and public gardens – or go for a boat-ride on the Nile. There is music, song and dance, covered at times by the roar of fireworks. Pedlars sell green branches of chick peas, endive, grilled corn, sweet potatoes and salted peanuts. Onions play a preponderant and unusual role in this celebration: one smells their scent on awakening and hangs bunches over the entrance of the home, and then smears their juice on the doorstep. These rites, strictly observed from one end of Egypt to the other, date back to a very remote era. Onions had a place in the ritual of certain pharaonic feasts: they were offered to Osiris and the deceased, and they played a primordial role in the annual feast of Sokar, the funerary divinity of Memphis.

Modern thought and art

The European influence that spread over Egypt during the nineteenth century brought an end to the traditional social and economic framework of the country. The sending of study groups to Europe, the installation of foreign schools, the translation of foreign works into Arabic, the birth of a modern free press, the development of painting, the arrival of Europeans (especially after 1860) – all these factors had a considerable impact. They brought profound changes to the country's cultural conceptions and social attitudes, which until that time had been homogeneous. An intense ferment of ideas, a profound political and social upheaval shook and stimulated Egyptian society, giving birth to the new, national, liberal culture of modern Egypt. In the beginning only a small privileged class profited by these events, but their effects gradually extended to all the population. The challenges of progress invested even the stronghold of religious tradition, the university of al-Azhar, where among the Ulemas there were men who accepted it with courage. One of these pioneers, Rifar al-Tahtawi, is the first historian to emphasize the permanence and continuity of Egypt, "mother of the nations of the world," and to distinguish between Umma (the community of believers) and Watan (nation-state) by declaring that every national society must have freedom, interpreted as equal rights and duties for all, as its basis. Towards the end of the century a Syrian-Lebanese colony of political refugees from the Ottoman oppression settled in the major centres and played a leading role in the Egyptian "renaissance," thanks to the dynamism of the intellectuals, journalists and writers.

In those spheres where there was no tradition in Arabic literature – such as the novel, the short story, the epic and the theatre – the influence of Europe was decisive. The first novel translated by Tahtawi in 1950, *Les Aventures de Télèmaque* by Fénelon, was followed by *Paul et Virginie*. The most sought-after works were English and French stories of love and adventure, which were soon imitated and plagiarised. In 1870 Osman Galal translated three tragedies by Racine and four comedies by Molière into the vernacular. Theatrical companies sprang up, performing in all the popular quarters. The Cairo Opera presented works in French and classical Arabic from the European repertory. Between 1919 and 1936 the Romantics were in vogue; Yusuf Wahbi and Rosa al-Yusuf played in *Cyrano de Bergerac, L'Aiglon*, and *La Dame aux camélias* with great success. But it was popular theatre that enjoyed the most remarkable success, due especially to the use of dialect and to the talent of two men, Badie Khairi and Nagib al-Rihani, the latter gifted with extraordinary talent as an actor, who served up witty and frivolous foreign pieces in such a thoroughly Egyptian sauce that they appeared genuine.

As for poetry, its solidly established tradition limited innovation. It was engaged at that time in a return to the sources, the most eminent representative of which was Ahmad Chawki, crowned the "Prince of Poets" in 1927.

An Egyptian literature properly so called, at once genuine and modern, emerged gradually. Although the new poetry, in the style of the French Romantics, limited itself to amorous confidences, the theatre began to exalt nationalism and Egyptian identity. Specialised magazines published short stories, a highly valued literary genre destined to have a brilliant future, whose technique, although still inspired by foreign writers, was applied to Egyptian society. To discover the latter, the more eminent writers chose the autobiographical mode. Perhaps the best of these writers was Taha Husayn (d. 1973), an outstanding figure to whom blindness gave an experience of suffering, sensitivity and modesty that enabled him to understand the life of his country. For him the future of culture in Egypt resided in the harmonious union of Eastern and Western civilisation. Tawfig al-Hakim (born in 1898), whose oeuvre is quite extensive, excells as a novelist (*Journal of a Country Substitute*) and playwright. Muhammad and Mahmud Taymur are also among the discoverers of society's tragedies and miseries, the former tending towards stories of the poor, the latter of the mystics.

Literary theatre with social content is dominated by Tawfig al-Hakim, the master of the genre. His first work in dialect caused such an outburst as to make him adopt a "middle" language – a sort of intermediate Arabic between the classical and the vernacular. He fills this very lively language with an intelligent and caustic spirit that clearly shows his mastery of the theatre.

Literature for the highly educated has gradually found an increasingly numerous audience. Writers of novels and short stories, in a remarkably incisive presentation of society, have brought to literature some of its more engaging qualities. These writers vary slightly in nuance and in their visions of reality. The two basic themes are the land – emphasizing the rift between the uneducated peasantry and the representatives of authority – and the patriarchal family. Abd al-Rahman al-Charkai (*The Land*), Yahya Hakki, Nagib Mahfuz (*Trilogy*, 1957), Yusuf Idris, Ihsan Abd al-Kuddus, Yusuf al-Sebai, and more recently, women writers – Nawwal al-Saadawi, Lutfiyya al-Zayyat and Bint al-Shati – are among the more outstanding representatives.

After the Second World War love was no longer sufficient subject matter for poets, who felt the need to turn to other sources, it being impossible to stand apart from the general movement. Breaking with love poetry, they took interest in the fate of the disinherited and in nationalism, to which they soon added socialism.

The creation of an avant-garde theatre and the information provided by the press regarding European literary criticism compelled socially concerned literature to yield to the cult of the irrational. The theatre of the absurd, for instance, finds echos in Tawfig al-Hakim and Yusuf Idris.

Moving away from the form and the rhyme of lyrical poetry, poets sought new rhythms. Salah Abd al-Sabbur, Ahmad Higazi and others adopted the stanza and the quatrain. Vernacular poetry, previously considered minor, developed after the fifties, especially in the work of Shawki and al-Tunsi.

The opening towards Europe enabled Egyptian society to experience and appreciate European artworks. After 1891 public squares were adorned with statues which would have been inconceivable a century earlier. Local artists remained indifferent for a long time. Then the younger generations became enthusiastic for the new art, and the first Fine Arts School was founded in 1908. Mahmud Mukhtar is the pioneer of the new school of sculpture. Famous for his monument *The Awakening of Egypt*, he established a direct rapport with pharaonic sculpture. Talented artists followed, including Gamal al-Seguini and Adam Henein, whose works approach the cubists' style.

The school of painting likewise prospered. Study groups were sent to Rome, where an Egyptian Academy was founded. Although the techniques were new, the artists drew their inspiration from the landscapes and scenes of daily life of their people. The best known of the elder painters are Mahmud Said, Muhammad Nagi (who shows impressionistic tendencies), Ahmad Sabri, Muhammad Hassan, Yusuf Kamil and Raghib Ayyad. Of the younger artists, Said Abd al-Rassul, Abd al-Hadi al-Gazar, Inji Aflatun, and others are doing good work.

Two genuine achievements that have received international acknowledgement deserve mention here. The first is the architectural work of two talented men, Hassan Fathi and Ramses Wissa Wassef. Resolutely turning their backs on the "international style," these two architects, professors in the School of Fine Arts, have created a style that reconciled the necessities of modern life with the climate, lifestyle and prestigious past of Egypt. They take account of aesthetics, comfort and economy, and maintain a strong tie with the past, by the use of brick domes and vaults handed down from the first pharaonic dynasties. Their best-known joint project is the village of Gurna opposite Luxor, on the west bank of the Nile.

The second original achievement is the art school created by Ramses Wissa Wassef at Harrania on the road to Sakkara. His faith in the gift of child creativity has led him to offer his young pupils the experience of direct improvisation in different media, as tapestry, while scrupulously respecting the autonomy of each artist and protecting it from everything that risks to destroy its genuineness. He has obtained some remarkable results. They have given rise to imitation throughout the country – some more successful than others – which today provide opportunities for young artists on a national scale.

CHAREH

149

150

51

152

148. Most streets in Cairo are really open-air markets.

149-150. The province of Fayyum has always been an important agricultural area. Through the creation of irrigation basins, land was reclaimed from the desert here as early as the 12th dynasty, around 1900 BC.

151-152. In the old city-centre of Cairo the digging of clay for making pots and the pottery workshops themselves still follow traditional methods.

153

15

155

153-154. Asyut is today the centre of the cotton industry. Egypt is the world's leading producer of cotton.

155. A factory of sun-baked bricks, in the province of Fayyum, used for building the houses in the countryside.

156

157

158

156. The agrarian reform, enacted after 1952, has produced remarkable results: Egyptian agriculture's yield of corn is equal to that of the United States.

157. The tapestries of the Ramsès Wissa Wassef art school, near the village of Harrania, are inspired by everyday scenes.

158. Fishermen along the Nile near El Saff.

159. Ploughing in a field on the road between Luxor and Dendera, on the east bank of the Nile.

159

160. Although one of the most spectacular aspects of the Sinai peninsula is the variety and brilliance of the colours of the rocks and minerals, the rocks shown here were in fact painted blue by an artist belonging to the Land Art movement.

162

163

164

161. Colourful fishing nets drying near the port of Damietta.

162. The population explosion of Cairo has forced some people to live in this cemetery.

163. A news kiosk in Luxor advertising its wares.

164. Dress materials on sale in a shop.

165 

166 

 16

165-171. Traditional colours and decorations. Those who have houses paint them; the Bedouins, being nomadic, wear their decorations.

68

169

170

71

172

173

172. View of the Sinai peninsula from across the Red Sea.

173. Barbed wire along the coastline of the Red Sea; this area is still controlled by the military.

174. Relics in the Sinai desert of one of the many wars fought over this area.

174

175

176

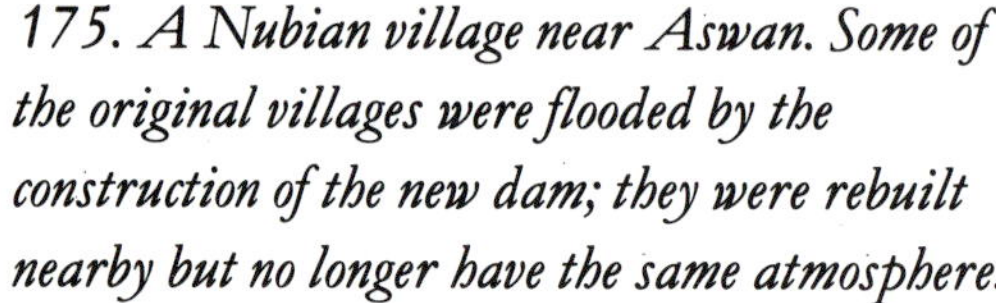

175. A Nubian village near Aswan. Some of the original villages were flooded by the construction of the new dam; they were rebuilt nearby but no longer have the same atmosphere.

176. An oil tanker on the Suez Canal.

177. The Aswan dam.

178. General view of Cairo.

177

178

179. Fishermen's boats on Lake Edku, in the delta.

180

180. The main square of modern Cairo, El Tahrir.

181. Today Cairo is a fascinating and disquieting city of brutal contrasts, in which ancient and modern monuments, poor and wealthy neighbourhoods stand side by side.

182. Street photographer in Luxor.

181

2

183

184

183. Nasser's portrait sill looks out from this wall near the Sultan Hassan mosque.

184. The shops of craftsmen – knife-grinders, tailors, basket-makers, barbers, mattress-carders, etc. – open directly onto the street and conceal little of their daily work.

185. Television helps pass the time while waiting for customers.

186. Traditional crafts are passed on from father to son.

185

Chronology

c. 6000 BC	NEOLITHIC PERIOD
c. 3600 BC	EARLY PREDYNASTIC PERIOD (Amratian culture)
c. 3300 BC	MIDDLE PREDYNASTIC PERIOD (Gerzean culture)
c. 3200 BC	LATE PREDYNASTIC PERIOD
c. 3000-2778 BC	THINITE KINGDOM (1st and 2nd dynasties)
	Menes/Narmer unites Upper and Lower Egypt and makes Memphis capital of the kingdom
2778-2263 BC	OLD KINGDOM (3rd-6th dynasties)
	Djoser constructs Step Pyramid at Sakkara Snefru sends expeditions to Nubia, Libya and Sinai Cheops, Khephren and Menkaure build the Pyramids of Giza
2263-2160 BC	FIRST INTERMEDIARY PERIOD (7th-10th dynasties)
	Rise of feudal power Division of the country between Theban and Heracleopolitan dynasties
2160-1785 BC	MIDDLE KINGDOM (11th and 12th dynasties)
	Mentuhotep I reunites the country with Thebes as his capital Amenemhet moves the capital to Memphis Land reclaimed in the Fayyum *The Story of Sinuhe*, *The Tale of a Peasant* and other classics of Egyptian literature written
1785-1580 BC	SECOND INTERMEDIARY PERIOD (13th-17th dynasties)
	The country is conquered by the Hyksos
1580-1085 BC	NEW KINGDOM (18th-20th dynasties)
	Ahmose defeats the Hyksos, founds the 18th dynasty and makes Thebes his capital Thutmosis I makes Nubia an Egyptian province and extends the empire into the Sudan Hatshepsut becomes co-regent with Thutmosis III and constructs her temple at Deir el Bahari Thutmosis III conquers Palestine and most of Syria Tombs built in the Valley of the Kings Colossi of Memnon built for the funeral temple of Amenophis III

	The schism of Aton: Amenophis IV changes his name to Akhenaton and moves his capital to Tell-el-Amarna in an effort to institute a monotheistic, sun-disk worship Hymns to the Sun written Tomb of Tutankhamen General Horemheb assumes power
	Ramses I founds the 19th dynasty Mortuary temple of Seti I at Abydos The Poem of Pentaur celebrates Ramses II's victory over the Hittites in 1278 BC Treaty of Tanis, between Egypt and the Hittites Temples of Karnak, Luxor, Abu Simbel and the Ramesseum
	Sethnakht founds the 20th dynasty Ramses III reorganises the administration and divides the population into classes Temple of Medinet Habu
1085-333 BC	LATE DYNASTIC PERIOD (21st-30th dynasty)
	Smendes founds the 21st dynasty making his capital at Tanis The Libyan prince Sheshouk founds the 22nd dynasty in 950 BC Tefnakte, prince of Sais, founds the 24th dynasty but is unable to prevent the loss of Upper Egypt to Kush The 25th Kushite dynasty gives Egypt fifty years of peace but finally falls to the Assyrians Psamtik I, King of Sais, expells the Assyrians and founds the 26th dynasty Cambyses, King of Persia, invades Egypt and proclaims himself pharaoh, founding the 27th dynasty The last three independent dynasties are overrun by the Persians once more in 341 BC
333-30 BC	THE MACEDONIAN ERA
	Conquest of Alexander the Great, greeted as a liberator by the Egyptians Ptolemy becomes king in 318 BC Institution of the state worship of the Sacred Bull of Apis Temples at Edfu and Dendera built Cleopatra IV, defeated at Actium, kills herself in 30 BC
30 BC - 640 AD	ROMAN AND BYZANTINE DOMINATION
	Temple of Isis on the island of Philae built Fayyum portraits, painted on wood The accession of Diocletian in 284 marks the beginning of Byzantine era Edict of Theodosius (392) forbids pagan rites
639-642	Arab conquest of Egypt
706	Arabic is made the official language
725	Coptic revolt
832	Copts defeated at the battle of Basharud
868-905	Tulunid rule
	Mosque of Ibn Tulun built
905-935	Abbasid rule
939-968	Ikshidite rule

969-1171	Fatimid rule
	Jauhar founds the city of al-Kahira, Cairo Mosques of al-Azhar and al-Hakim built
1171-1250	Ayyubite rule
1250-1381	Bahri Mameluke rule
	Mosque of Sultan Hassan built
1382-1517	Circassian Mameluke rule
	Mosque of al-Muayyad built
1517-1798	Ottoman rule
1798, July 1	Napoleon lands at Abukir
1801	The French, defeated by the British, withdraw from Egypt
1805	Mehmet Ali, having forced the British to withdraw and ousted the Mamelukes from power, is nominated Pasha of Egypt by the Sultan
1849	Abbas I becomes Pasha
1854-1863	Rule of Saïd
	Suez Canal begun
1863	Rule of Ismail begins
1867	Ismail granted title of Khedive
1869	Suez Canal inaugurated
1879	Tawfig succeeds Ismail, deposed by the Sultan
1882	France and Great Britain re-establish control over Egypt
1914	Egypt is declared a British protectorate
1922	Declaration of Egyptian independence
	Fuad becomes King of Egypt
1936	Fuad dies and is succeeded by his son Faruk
1937	Egypt is admitted to the League of Nations
1952, July 23	Military coup makes Egypt a republic with General Naguib as President
1954	Gamal Abdel Nasser becomes President
1970	Nasser dies and is succeeded by Anwar Sadat
1981, October 6	Sadat is assassinated
	Mubarak becomes President